THE HOUND OF HEAVEN

NO MAN CAN SERVE TWO MASTERS

J. A. Rispoli

PULPO
PUBLISHING

New York

ISBN:978-1-7326418-2-2 (paperback)
ISBN: 978-1-7326418-1-5 (eBook)

Library of Congress Control
Number: 2018910051

Cover Illustration by James Madsen.
Cover Typography by Betsy Franco Feeney

Printed in the United States of America.

Adapted from the original screenplay *The Hound of Heaven* (formerly *God Only Knows*)

This novel does not conform to a belief that language which could offend political sensibilities should be eliminated—

Therefore, it is NOT POLITICALLY CORRECT, proceed at will.

PULPO
PUBLISHING

Pulpo Publishing

A division of

Otis Spo Productions, LLC
P.O. Box 393
Piermont, New York, 10968

thehoundofheavennovel.com

In honor of our loved ones…

…whose stories ended too soon.

PULPO
PUBLISHING

To Richard,
This may seem
familiar but it is fiction.
I hope you enjoy the book,
and I look forward to
your thoughts. Thank you!

Joseph A. Puzzoli

Table of Contents

"Oz never did give nothing to the Tin Man
that he didn't ... didn't *already* have."

~America

Intro

I'VE HEARD IT SAID, *GRACE*, doesn't see good or evil people... simply, people willing to receive it.

In a person's pursuit to find truth, purpose, straying into darkness, I believe, is inevitable. In fact, the very pursuit of it may be why it eludes so many. Perhaps it is *Truth, purpose,* that pursues you.

I heard a still small voice within years ago, when my mind was once quiet enough to listen. Wisdom perhaps. Because I sensed instantly, running from it could prove to be perilous. I listened to that conscious a majority of the time, and I'm glad I did.

Because, unexpectedly—I died.

Well, my body did anyway.

As a young boy when I first realized death was inevitable for us all, I imagined the best way to go would be in my sleep. A beloved old man, after a full life. That didn't happen.

Because one thing that's certain in life is, well, uncertainty.

The following page begins a young man's story. His journey, through the seen and the unseen. His challenges, his choices, his strengths, and weaknesses—his dreams and demons.

I live on through this young man, as some believe spirits, or those dearest to you do. Because, he's my son, my oldest, Nick. I remember the day he was born, like it was yesterday. And he clearly remembers that day I died— much clearer than me.

He had the better view.

Chapter One

Knocking on Heaven's Door

"It's gettin' dark, too dark to see…"

~ Bob Dylan

September, 1976

"Nicholas!" Wrapping a towel around my waist, I crack the bathroom door.

"Yeah Ma?" The smell of simmering garlic, basil, and tomato fill my nose, like every Sunday.

"Gina called when you were showering, she'll be over within the hour."

"Okay. Thanks, Ma." I run my fingers through my hair as I cross the carpeted hall to my room. I'm not surprised to see my little brother Joey in it.

"Could I borrow your catcher's mitt?" His brown eyes plead above a curious smile.

"The one you're wearing?" He knows I'll say yes.

"Dad's gonna throw me some pitches." Smacking it with his fist.

"Yeah. Just put it back where you found it."

"Guess who I have for homeroom this coming year?" Like it's some juicy secret, he's gonna be ten soon.

"Homeroom? I don't know. Who?" I'm thirteen, and we teenagers never talk grammar school in junior high.

"Mom says you had her in fourth grade too."

"Miss Nevins?" I flip through an envelope of photos I pulled from my dresser.

"Yup. Got her for religion class too."

"So did I. She's a real sweet lady." I give a slight smack on the back of his head. "So behave."

He slaps me harder and sprints for the door. "See you outside, thanks!"

3

"Hey, wait a minute..." He stops shy of the doorway. "Gina and I want to take you out for your birthday next month, our treat."

"Yeah! Coool. Out to where?" His eyes widen, brows rising into his forehead.

"We were thinking either the movies, the roller rink or bowling. You pick."

"Can Patricia come?" he asks sincerely. *I didn't expect that.*

"Yeah uh, okay sure. But you'll need to ask mom first about her." Our sister *Trisha* is twelve, but needs to go to a different school on a special bus.

"Mom will let her go to a movie, I think." he says. "Yeah a matinee, thanks, big brother! Gotta go, Pop's waiting." He bolts out the door.

The photos I'm flipping through, my father took a few months ago at my Confirmation. They sat in my drawer all summer. I pull out one of Gina and me in our ceremonial robes on the church steps. We're waving, smiling at the camera. I put it aside on top of my bureau to make her a copy. Here's one, my Pop and just me smiling proud. He's squeezing his sturdy arm around my shoulder. I'm taping this one to my mirror. And… this one of the family that Gina took that day, I'm gonna frame for my mom. I slip the rest back into my dresser drawer for a photo album.

I throw on my favorite jeans and a T-shirt and send a comb through my hair. I make my bed and give a few good sweeps under it with a dust mop, which extracts Snicker bar wrappers, my Bob Dylan cassette, some lint, a dusty sock, and a quarter. With one last swipe, a baseball rolls out from the corner and stops under my window. I put the Dylan tape back in my cassette case next to a stack of albums. One day I'm gonna record my favorite songs onto one cassette.

The quarter is a Bicentennial coin. Special print, 1776- 1976, that came out this year. I put it into my bowl of odd coins to add to the collection my Dad, Joey, and I have.

The scent of sweet Italian sausage searing with braised beef now reaches the second floor. The aroma blending with her sauce has seeped under my door, into my room. My stomach growls in anticipation of Sunday's family meal. The cornflakes before church isn't cutting it anymore.

"Nicholas!" I swing open my door

"Yeah Mom, what's up?" My question echoes down the empty stairwell.

"Can you give me a hand down here please?" she asks.

"Okay, sure. Just straightening up my room."

"I need you to bread the eggplant your father picked this morning."

"Okay, be right down." I gently shake the dust mop into my waste basket.

Within that moment, I focus on a ray of sunlight that cuts through my window lighting up a stream of tiny floating dust particles. There's thousands drifting and rotating in the sunbeam. I'm still, yet they move. I gaze closely. When outside the suns ray, they simply disappear. One second they're there and the next, they *seem* gone.

"Me Joey, ME! Me Joey, ME!" I hear my sister Trisha's voice from outside.

Through my second-floor window I see her on the front lawn in the shade of the big oak tree. She's waiting for Joey to throw her the baseball. He's in the middle of catching with my Dad.

"Okay...okay Trisha, just a minute. You get the next one." I hear him say.

"Hey Sis, over here. Up here." I say in a raised voice as I stick my head out the window. I revolve the baseball I found in my fingers.

"Hi, Nicky!" she runs, in her awkwardness, towards me.

"Hey Buddy." My Dad calls from across the lawn.

"Yeah Pop?"

"Did you see the size of those eggplant I picked today?"

His thick dark hair, broad shoulders, smiling eyes, and face remind me of Dean Martin. I hope I grow as tall as him. People say I look just like him when he was my age.

"The eggplant? Not yet. I'm heading down to help mom now." My voice cracks.

It's changing. Weird. Going through some changes.

"Okay squeaky," he says with a wide grin. I look back to Trisha.

"Hey Trisha, watch! Okay ready? …Here you go, catch!"

I gently toss the ball underhand to her and it drops right before her mitt and rolls between her legs, catching the downgrade of the lawn. It gradually picks up speed, rolling toward the sidewalk. She turns following it, the best she can. *C'mon get it Trish, get it!*

She's determined, keeping her 'eye on the ball,' unaware; it's heading right over the sidewalk and into the road. Even though we play in the road all the time, she's not allowed even to cross the street without us.

"DAD! Hey, Dad. Can you get Trisha!" From across the lawn, he turns to face her.

My eyes shift up the street and see our very quiet road being invaded by the huge grill of a cherry red Mack flatbed, a tow truck. It's barreling up our block. I can see the driver reacting. His eyes enlarge and his nostrils flare as he wrestles with the wheel with nowhere to turn on this tree-lined street. Panic fills his face. His body lurches back as he stamps on the brakes. Trisha, now in the street and in the truck's path, freezes at the blast of his air horn. Staring just yards away from the Mack truck's grill. The brakes are now squealing, screeching, as I yell loudly again. DAD! Trisha!

My Dad's on it, throwing his glove down, and running towards her. The driver blasts its air horn again. My father's sudden steps toward immediate danger invade me. I tremble, seeing his worried expression, as he sprints across the lawn and into the street. Trisha upright and rigid is still facing the oncoming truck.

Its wheels are squealing, horn still blasting, as it's now bucking, hopping, trying to stop. A nauseous feeling comes over me as my stomach tightens and twists.

He reaches her! Gripping Trisha and placing himself between the truck and her, he lunges, releasing her safely onto a neighbor's lawn. She's crying, wailing loudly.

The full impact of the truck strikes him so hard his head bounces off the huge chrome grill. His body follows as he's thrown several feet before the truck comes to a complete stop. He lays limp, distorted, and lifeless on the road, in his church clothes. Joey's body stiffens, my baseball mitt slides off his hand onto the grass. My hands instinctively cover my eyes, protecting my mind from an unimaginable scene.

"Noooo! Dad, Nooo!" Joey's voice pierces my ears. Snapping me back. I see him standing, still frozen. His face is draining color, staring wide-eyed at our Dad. I can see he's wetting his pants. A growing red pool leaks onto the pavement around my father. Neighbors step out onto their lawns, women scream as men, helpless, gather by him. My mom runs into the street and kneels at his side bending down into his ear then looking skyward, praying, crying, rocking, before leaning down again speaking into his ear.

I fly down the stairs and bolt out the door crossing over to Trisha. Hoping to quiet her. Trisha suddenly gazes to the street where my Dad lies. Her wailing begins to calm as she's catching her breath, sniffling, and suddenly stops. She's staring with wide-eyed awe, towards my Mom and Dad. Her gaze lifts upward in childlike wonder pointing up into the rays of the sun passing through the oak tree and then far above it. Her eyebrows rise, as her astonished look becomes a wide smile. She giggles.

"I called an ambulance!" Some neighbor yells as she steps out of her house.

The truck driver steps down from the cab. His bewildered look, sunken stature and sorrowful eyes speak such sadness. He steps slowly towards my Mom and Dad, stopping several yards short of them.

My sister is still smiling and giggling, as I'm about to scream out loud, in front of everyone. I hold it in. *Her issues must be deeper than we think. Why did I even throw her the ball?*

Gina cycles up on her bike and stops suddenly in front of a neighbor's house. She slides off her seat and straddles the bike, gripping the handlebars. Seeing the scenario, her mouth drops open; she quickly covers it with her hand. I see what she sees. My Dad's lifeless body on the pavement, my Mom hovered over him crying. His head rests bloodied on her apron between her knees. Joey stands alone, sobbing. I want to help him.

I'm past light-headed, I'm dizzy. My muscles feel limp and my surroundings begin to spin. Strength seems to be draining from me. I'm having a hard time focusing and holding up my head. I swing it back over to Gina. Her beautiful eyes tearfully meet mine. Trisha awkwardly runs, with her arms out to embrace her.

My eyes fill, fogging my vision until they leak down my cheeks. Joey's scream seems distant, fading. My legs become jelly, I sense myself collapsing, folding onto the grass. My eyes slowly begin rolling up into the deep darkness of my mind.

Chapter Two

I'm Eighteen

"I'm in the middle without any plans,
I'm a boy and I'm a man…"

~ Alice Cooper

THE GOWN I WEAR SEEMS big enough to shoplift a six-pack. And I don't feel too good about the vandalism I'm here to do. All the doubt that dogged me that I wouldn't make it this far is behind me. I'm thrilled about today, my Graduation Day. I am free from the regimen and rules in this place. Other people's authority over my life never sat well with me since my Dad died five years ago. But there's something I need to do, to carry on a tradition of past senior classes dating back to the late 60s.

And this will be my last chance.

I swing open the door and the smell of mildewed showers and stale smoke hits me hard. I pull my headphones out, reach into my gown and blindly push the play button on my *Walkman* as I enter the boys locker room for the last time. The first time I entered it, *I was* just a boy, a freshman with a couple of years of puberty under my belt. I just started getting high and was steady with Gina for two years already. Juniors and seniors were going all the way with their girlfriends and they'd tease the hell out of me that we weren't.

The opening notes of *I'm Eighteen*, play clearly in my mind. The beat of Alice Cooper fills it to the point that my head rocks. The song seems to echo throughout the locker room and I feel filled with the deep vibes of it, like I'm walking on air into a movie set or something. Back in March, I played this song a thousand times, confirming my eighteen-year milestone, I'm a man now.

Not only could I get drafted, but I could also smoke, drink legally or move out and get my own place.

I could vote, but I don't see the use. After watching Woodstock and the Vietnam War on TV as a kid, I bet my vote wouldn't even matter. Peace isn't profitable for the guys running things.

Every locker in this place has been emptied and the room is literally trashed. I kick through old sneakers, headbands, cleats and jockstraps. The custodians it seems steered clear of here the last few days, knowing that some graffiti is certain; it has been for years.

There's not a soul in sight as I pull out an extra-wide black marker and write "Disco's Dead" then draw a skull and cross bones next to it. Right beneath it, in caps, I put "Bon Scott Lives!" Even though he died last year, choked on his vomit. But the music lives on. Above it, I pen "AC/DC" in large letters and draw a large lightning bolt next to it.

I want to scrawl my last name "Anselmo" across the lacquered wooden locker-room bench but that's a sure bust, so I just turn and sit on it instead. I look around at the art, some real talent, much of it only a few days old. There're photo albums of each year somewhere in the school archives I've heard. Graffiti is not my thing, but I just had to do this; it's tradition.

On my right, I see "Lemmon 714," the Quaalude, still the pill of choice.

"Eat Me I'm a Twinkie" is scrawled on the coach's office window. Word around school is he may be one. I stand up and wander past "Smoke Cannabis" written in green across three lockers. A huge pot leaf and "Hendrix Rocks!" follow it. I see southern rock groups have been honored this year across the locker room walls with a confederate flag painted on one. A very welcome *Rebel* invasion over the last few years. Seems odd for a school in the suburbs of New York City full of Yankee fanatics. *"Molly Hatchet," "Skynyrd," "Allman Brothers"* and *"ZZ top"* are written right next to *"Yankees Rule," "Boston Sucks," "Go Reggie"* and *"The Outlaws."*

Then I see the iconic pair of lips and lapping tongue, painted in

12

bright red. One of my favorites, the Rolling Stones logo from their "Sticky Fingers" album. Man, that would make a cool tattoo.

I head into the sink and vanity area and see Led Zeppelin's Swan Song Records logo drawn onto the ceiling above me, reflected in the mirror above the sink. I look up in awe at Icarus's head tilted back, arms raised as he seems to rise with outstretched wings. It's detailed and in full color. I imagine it had to take a couple of hours. It's gonna really suck when they paint over that one. I wish I had a camera; I'd love to show it to Gina. That Swan Song logo would make an even cooler tattoo.

I think of Zeppelin's drummer, John Bonham, and how he passed out drunk and choked to death on his puke last year too. Crazy. I hear now you just need to take one of those Quaaludes and it feels like you drank three six-packs or a half a bottle of liquor.

I look in the mirror and see my Dad in me. I'm the same height now, broad shouldered, brown eyes, sharp chin, and a dimple. Except my hair is far from his neat short slick cut. Mine is more like David Cassidy, in The Partridge Family. I place the blue square cap with the yellow tassel on my head and pull my hair back under my cap. I take out a single diamond-stud earring from a small box and insert it into my left ear. Every time my girlfriend, Gina, trimmed my hair she'd talk about piercing my ear. She finally broke me down and a couple of days ago I agreed.

The earring's a tenth wedding anniversary gift from my Dad to my Mom, she lost one last year so I asked her for this one to see if Gina and I could find a match at the mall. We couldn't find one.

I let my hair down again and it's hidden a bit. I like it. It's from my Dad and was just sitting in her jewelry box. I hope she lets me keep it for now. Not sure how Dad would've felt about an earring on me though; I'm pretty sure he'd disagree if he were alive. The only earrings on men he probably saw in his life were on Gypsies,

Pirates, and Genies. And only on TV I'm sure. I hate to think of it, but I know there are several things I'd disagree with him on now. But the times they are a-changing

I reach under my graduation gown and pull out a pint of black-berry brandy from an inside pocket and take a swig. I head for the exit and push the cross bar with the bottom of my foot; swinging the steel door wide open to a panoramic scene. A huge assembly of my fellow graduates on the school football field, over four hundred of us this year. I see they raised a large banner above the stage that reads "Congratulations Hudson Valley Graduating Class of 1981."

I look around at the stands packed with people as beach balls bounce off the heads and hands of my fellow graduates on the center of the field. My ears tune to the crowd and I feel an electric buzz up the back of my neck as I hear firecrackers popping off and Alice Cooper still jamming in my head.

Some of the senior girls are passing a bottle of peppermint Schnapps between them, toasting themselves a bit early. There are hundreds of graduates, I remove my headphones as I move down to the middle rows and slip into the seat next to my buddies. Seems no teachers even knew I was missing. Not the only one in a cap and gown with long hair. It's not rock-star long or 60's hippies long, but shoulder length, still too long for my mom's liking.

At this point, nothing really matters, not much the teachers can do. They've been outnumbered all year. We are one of the last and largest classes left from the "Baby Boom." I've heard that more than once from them.

I stand for a few seconds and take a quick look in the stands for my Mom and Uncle Lou. They're somewhere up there in the bleachers with my little brother and sister, and a couple of cousins. I give up immediately, it's just so crowded.

My Dad's been gone for over five years now, and I suddenly miss him terribly. I get that every so often. My heart drops to my stomach, and I'll feel a bit sick remembering it. I usually just get buzzed or stoned and try to forget it. In fact, it seems lately, sleeping may be the only time that I'm not a little buzzed.

I sit down between my friends and I pass the bottle of blackberry brandy to my buddy Pauly. He's been stocky ever since I met him in grade school. And since then he seems to find trouble easily. I see he's handing a joint secretively to Frankie, another good buddy of mine since day one in grade school.

"Hey, did you do it man? Did you tag your locker?" Pauly asks.

"Yeah. Yeah... I did."

What'd you put?"

"Wrote 'Discos Dead', 'AC/DC' and couple of other things."

"Did you see the Swan Song on the ceiling? I heard Vitelli drew that" he says.

"Did he really? Great talent in there this year."

Pauly swigs the brandy, grimacing, lifting his eyes to mine.

"I wish we had those pot brownies you made in Home Ec dude. Remember? They were killer."

He looks to a couple of teachers standing on the outskirts of the crowd looking around.

"I think they smell the weed. Brownies would have been better," he says.

I do remember. Thankfully, the Home Ec teacher was clueless and couldn't put a finger on the strange smell. She called maintenance thinking it was an electrical issue. The custodian could have told on us; he knew it right away. But he was no narc. A cool older Jamaican dude that I'm sure partied a little himself.

I took Home Economics because I love to cook, but it was never considered macho enough for my friends. So, I didn't tell them it was my choice. Those brownies were risky. I don't know why I did

15

it. A friend's sister, a senior that year gave me the recipe. I always like to experiment with food, and well, the smiles on my friend's faces were worth the risk.

My Mom's my inspiration to cook, she's the reason I applied to the best culinary school in the country. Less than an hour upstate it's a tough school to get into. Strict. Serious about only graduating the best chefs. My application has all I need to get in. Good references, a couple years of working kitchens, the high tuition, even though things have been tight. It's my high school transcripts and cutting out that concerns me. Pauly slaps my shoulder.

"Hey Nick. When you get out of that school for cooks, or whatever, I want the scoop on that spa, motel place you always talk about. I'll be your partner."

Frankie exhales and hands the joint over to me.

"It's not a motel dude. And get real, Pauly. I need an honest partner. Someone serious. And its really big bucks, a big plan. I'm doing it with Gina."

"Why'd you take "Home Ec" anyway?" Frankie asks.

"Because it was that or typing class. I'm no secretary dude and you know I like to cook."

"Hey, you know Patsy's making some pretty big bucks selling a ton of weed since he dropped out. Maybe he could back you." Pauly says.

"Forget about it Pauly. Friggin Patsy. You kidding me?"

A kid behind us taps Pauly on the shoulder, slyly motioning to get a swig of the brandy.

Pauly, handing it over secretively suddenly pulls it back.

"Psyche! Ha ha, hehe, just kiddin' bro…"

Then as he turns, he squints at the earring behind my hair.

"What the… are you serious? What's with the earring dude? I knew it, I knew it - you're turning fem on us," Pauly quips.

"Yeah Pauly, that's it, I'm fem. I've been thinking a lot about it and yeah, I decided I was a fag last night. You chump…" *As if people, can just wake up and be gay.*

"It does look pretty weird though," Frankie says, slowly shaking his head. "If you weren't so steady with Gina… I don't know…" Frankie slaps his forehead and adds: "Wait, you're cooking and crocheting in Home Ec. And you like it? Your words! What the hell is a frigging "spa" thing anyway?"

He looks closer at the earring for clues.

"Maybe you ARE a fem. A closet roller disco queen, taking dance classes too." He adds. Not like him. He's usually pretty quiet.

"That's it, keep thinking Frankie. Yeah, I'm a disco queen, moron."

"Yeah maybe you switch hit and you love Elton John," Pauly chimes in. "Maayybe… you could shave your head and put in a hoop, like Mr. Clean or something."

"Shut up retard, you talk too much."

"Mr. Clean is no faggot." Frankie coughs out after hitting the joint. "And neither is Elton John, I mean he wrote 'Benny and the Jets.'"

"How would you know; they don't talk about that crap. He's so high on drugs anyway. "Remember his clothes in the movie *Tommy*?" asks Pauly.

"He's gay dude, like Uncle Ernie in that movie is," he adds.

"Uncle Ernie was a pervert. Not gay dude." Frankie says.

"Yeah, right. Whatever. But I'm telling you, they don't talk about that crap." Pauly repeats.

"He's bisexual, I heard." I say, remembering a Rolling Stone interview years ago. He admitted it. Said he thinks everyone is…"

"Told you, switch-hitter," Pauly confirms. "And I'm pretty sure Springsteen is too. Jersey jerk. Nothing good comes from Jersey.

We toke on the joint and pass the bottle as they do a sound check on the stage up front.

"Testing, testing…1…2…" is heard clearly across the field.

"I'm psyched for Lisa's grad party tonight. I heard there are three kegs, and I bet over a hundred chicks will be there." Frankie says.

He turns and high fives Pauly with a loud smack.

"Kegs, bones, and babes in bikinis, awesome!" exclaims Pauly.

In the front of the assembly on a raised platform is our principal Mr. Hastings, who has been a mentor and great teacher to… well, none of us. We have no idea what he's said for the last fifteen minutes. He's standing at a podium calling out names one by one, handing out diplomas.

"Nicholas Anselmo." Hastings announces my name.

I'm taken by surprise and suddenly pushed hard by Pauly as I quickly stand up. I'm getting a serious head rush and feel a bit dizzy. Pauly starts prodding me in my side.

"Cool it." I say.

"You gonna say it dude, right? Just like you said you would, right? Come on man do it, do it Nick. It'll be so cool," he insists excitedly.

I know what he wants.

"I don't know dude, really… don't think so," I say. I receive pats on my back and ass as I slip through the row of fellow graduates.

"Come on Nick." Pauly pleads.

The line to the stage moves fairly quickly, and I'm still pretty buzzed when I step up to the podium.

With a wide grin, I ignore the extended hand of Mr. Hastings and look out to the crowd instead. I've spent some time in his office and caught him picking his nose and that just grosses me out. It makes me flashback to when I was talking to Susan Miller in 1st grade and she pulled snot out of her nose, looked at it, then ate it right in front of me; it made me gag.

"Congratulations Nicholas!" Mr. Hastings says to me, as I now make eye contact.

18

"I'm ready for the world Mr. H."

"I believe you are, I just hope the world is ready for you."

"Well, ready or not, hello world! See ya, Mr. Hastings."

I suddenly think of Pauly and my buzz overcomes my inhibitions. I quickly lean into the microphone and say in a deep voice…

"Luke… I am your Father."

Pauly screams out "yeah duuude!" over the laughter of the audience.

With a sudden rush of excitement, I raise up the diploma in my fist, lean in again to the mic and say cool, calmly…

"May the force be with you!"

"Okay that's enough son." Mr. Hastings quickly pulls the mic stand towards him while nervously filling one nostril with his left pinky finger.

"Later Mr. Hastings… pick me a winner."

Stepping down from the podium I feel like a rock star as I look out over my class and hear some cheering from the crowd.

Catching up with my Mom and family after the ceremony was easy cause my little brother cut right through the crowd leading them right to me. The beam on my mom's face greets me, she's thrilled. Hugging me, squeezing tight.

"Nickeee. I'm so proud of you!" her embrace feels great… it's been a while.

"That was so cool – 'Luke, I am your Father.'" My brother Joey cuts in quickly, with a big smile.

"'Luke, I am your Father'. Hahaha." he says again.

He imitates me all the time. *Not a good thing, if he keeps it up.*

"Yeah, Nicky." My Mom cuts in. "Where did that come from? You're lucky they let you graduate still," she says sternly.

"It was Pauly's idea. They don't care Mom. It was funny. Come on, you gotta admit."

"If Pauly said, 'let's jump off a bridge,' would that be a good idea too?" she added.

"Your principal wasn't thrilled with that last comment I'm sure."

"Come on Ma, everyone knows he's a jerk," I said.

"Well I know, but that's not nice to say about Pauly."

"I was talking about Hastings." I laugh. She just burned Pauly.

"Well you should know. You spent enough time in his office"

I smile. Just got burned by my Mom as well. Good one.

Uncle Lou steps towards me and extends his right hand, wrapping his left arm around my neck and shoulders.

"Congrats nephew, you did it. You have a bright future kid. Don't screw it up."

My sister Patricia walks up and nudges me with her body. My Mom says her strawberry blonde hair is from her father's side. It ends right above the lace neckline on her favorite blue dress she wears constantly.

"Hey Nicky!" She looks to me with cheery blue eyes. I rarely see her eye to eye because of the condition she has. She has trouble keeping eye contact with people for some reason.

"Here Nicky, I drew you a picture." I receive her sheet of paper.

"Hey, wow… okay yeah, thanks Trisha."

She carries a small sketchpad whenever she goes out of the house. At home, she could listen to old music, the Beatles, and do jigsaw puzzles all day long. She's a couple of years younger and was born with some mental condition; they're calling "autism." She's distant at times, in another world. Kinda stuck at an age of someone several years younger than her age of fifteen. She loves to draw, but her pictures of spirits, ghosts, and religious imaginary stuff, sometimes freak me out.

She points to it and says, "These bubbles floating up at the top over here are the angels. They want us to look up, towards them, and heaven."

I look at the picture and I see several clear orbs floating in front of the sun, with the clouds and birds.

"Oh, mmm, very interesting Trisha, yeah," I say.

In the center frame of the page, it looks like the graduating class with about a dozen students standing, looking up towards the orbs and sky, out of the hundreds that are still seated surrounding them.

"The people standing are among the living, believing, receiving it all," she tells me.

By now I just want to blow her off. I love her dearly but, like I said, it kinda freaks me out. And she's bringing me down from my buzz. She points to the drawing again and I see beneath the graduating class, a third of the page is shaded black with pencil across the whole bottom.

"Below, is where the rest live, because they only see the world and stuff... Never happy... never enough... Living in the dark."

"Oh, okay sure, that's great Trisha, thanks." I feel so sorry for her. My Mom steps in.

"We need to get going, your cousins will be by in a little while for your dinner tonight."

****

I can smell the escarole simmering in chicken stock distinctly as I enter the house. For every one of our birthdays, awards, or milestones my Mom would prepare whatever we wanted for dinner. She's a huge influence in my wanting to be a chef. I've been helping her in the kitchen since I was five. Over the years, I've picked up her style and secrets. The many flavors of the Mediterranean she learned from my grandmother. Traditional foods I learned were birthed out of poverty. Many of her dishes originated in Naples and were handed down through generations. They never failed to please anyone who was fortunate enough to be served by her.

She darts off to the kitchen.

"Ma, can I give you a hand?"

"No, I'm fine. You relax. It's your special day," she says, but I know she could use one.

Tonight, she's cooking a couple of my favorites. One is her 'Easter soup.' Some call it Italian wedding soup. It's made with fresh escarole, chicken, tiny meatballs, and eggs scrambled with Parmesan dropped in to cook at the end. It's so good topped with grated Romano and fresh ground black pepper.

It's usually only made once a year for Easter Day, cause it's quite the process. She uses capons for the stock because the flavor of the rooster is richer. Sometimes she skips the beef and pork and uses a rooster in the Sunday gravy during the summer, it's not as heavy.

She's sure to need help with the tiny meatballs for the soup today. She insists you have to be able to fit at least couple on a spoon along with the other ingredients. Even just a pound and a half of chopped meat could take an hour alone it seems.

It's definitely the most anticipated dish every Easter Sunday next to the baked Easter breads she makes. Like her lard bread with peppery bits of pork, or her spinach, sausage and provolone rolled into a crusty bastone loaf. But my favorite is her pizzagaina, a very rich bread. It's the meats and cheese you'd find in a good Italian combo. Cappicola, prosciutto, genoa salami, pepperoni, and provolone all diced and mixed into an egg and cream mixture, like a quiche, with grated Locatelli cheese and poured into a deep pan lined with bread dough that seals it in. Long and slow it cooks until the crust is a golden brown. And like the soup, it's even better the next day.

Asking for the bread would have been asking too much. And after following her into the kitchen into a wall of heat, I'm glad I didn't.

"Oh man, wow… it's hot in here." I say, opening a window, which doesn't help one bit as it's eighty-seven degrees out.

I open the oven and a wave of heat delivers a whiff of rosemary as I lean down to check out the lamb shanks slow roasting in the center of the oven.

"Hey ma, I'm really sorry. Ya know I would've been fine with some quick linguine and calamari or mussels fra diavlo or something."

I notice a stock simmering on the stove, I stick my head closer and wave my hand over it towards my face; it's distinct earthy aroma tells my nose it's porcini stock. It's for the mushroom risotto I requested as well as the shanks.

"This is what you wanted and that's fine with me. It's not every day that you graduate."

She places another pan on the stove and pours olive oil in it.

"Now hand me the broccoli rabe and quickly peel me some garlic please." She brushes stray hair from her brow with her forearm, "Then go visit with your uncle. Your cousins should be here soon."

I open the fridge and it's packed as usual. I rummage through and take out the broccoli rabe and hand it to her.

A sudden smile comes to me, recalling a time when I was thirteen, I laugh out loud.

"What's so funny?" Mom asks.

"Remember after that wrestling match, you took us out to eat with my friends, and Frankie thought ravioli came from cans?"

"Oh yes…that poor boy. That was a shame. *Chef Boyardee* and *Spaghetti O's*," she says, shaking her head.

"Hey Ma, how come we never got TV dinners?"

"Because it's nonsense. Who knows what's in those boxes and cans?

23

She's right, who knows what's in that stuff.

She gently pours porcini broth into the Arborio rice and shallots sautéing in olive oil and butter. It starts audibly simmering; the sound fades to silence as she gently stirs in more of the liquid and the risotto absorbs it. It will have to be added little by little to get the creamy texture it's famous for. The dish came from her grandmother, who cooked in a tiny Trattoria in Milan.

But no Italian restaurant can top my mom's cooking. Chinese food, or an American diner would be fine to go to, but the thought of someone else's marinara would give me an instant guilt trip. We were taught to respect food. And never serve something you wouldn't eat yourself or approve of. I've been working in kitchens the last few years with guys who didn't like, or eat things they were serving. I don't understand how they could do that.

As mom rinses the broccoli rabe, I hit the garlic cloves with the side of my knife to separate the skin.

"Hey Honey, remember your Dad used to take us every so often to the Hawaiian Luau restaurant, with that huge smorgasbord of food?" I clearly recall that place.

"Yes, of course, I remember, I loved that place," I say and she smiles.

I did love that place. We stopped going because it wasn't easy with Trisha's handicap. But that place opened my mind to an eastern world of flavors. I saw ingredients and techniques I never would have experienced at home. They did squid very different from the Italians and, well… everything else… beef, chicken, shrimp, and pasta. I would fill up on their duck, something my mom would never make, as it was "too fatty".

It wasn't long after our last time at the smorgasbord that I read in a magazine that American cuisine was competing with the French.

I wanted in, to learn more about it.

The traditional French and Italian places that dominated the restaurant scene would have to make room for new American chefs. When I read about that, it excited me because it was happening now. I look up from the cutting board towards my mom.

"Is this enough garlic?" I go to hand her the bowl.

"Yes, plenty. Just give it a rough chop for me will you please?"

I slide the cloves out onto the cutting board and pick up the knife.

"Yeah that buffet place was great," I say. My Mom stops and turns eagerly to me.

"I know! We should all go together again before you head off to school."

"That's a good idea…yeah." We haven't gone anywhere as a family in a long time, I realize. My free time has been filled with parties and friends.

I slide the chopped garlic back into the bowl and place it by my mom.

"Thanks Honey. The Hawaiian Luau will be exciting. You can get the duck, Remember?"

"Yeah it's been a while, sounds good." I rinse my hands off in the sink and kiss her on the cheek. "I'm gonna go visit with Uncle Lou a minute. I'll be back to help finish up."

"Good idea. No worries Honey, I'm in good shape, thank you."

I turn and see she really is on top of things. Standing in her white frilled apron, hair up, loose ends frame her face as she cuts the stem bottoms from the broccoli rabe.

I think to myself, *is she forty or forty-one? Wow, she's getting old.* Even though most people think she's in her early thirties. She'd probably be fitting for the cover of *Good Housekeeping* magazine. I could just see it, Angelina Anna Maria Anselmo's recipes inside. She'd blow away Julia Child with her modern Italian mom look and charm.

She's juggling a full oven and stovetop as she sautés, simmers and stirs soup. She is the queen of no stress multitasking. She's fine, has it covered. I'll jump in with the meatballs later. I'm just about out the door when she turns to me.

"You know Nicky, your father is very proud of you. Do you know what he told me when you were young?" Whoa where'd that come from?

I stop and turn. "No. Ma. What's that?"

"That you would be great at whatever you chose to do."

"He said that, huh?" I smile inside.

"Yes, he did."

My brother Joey enters the kitchen from the back porch.

"Take those boots off," my mom says immediately.

He turns around all muddy and sweaty. He plays hard with his dirt bike. He's fourteen and a really good kid. His friends are all good kids, far from the stuff I was already into at that age. He looks up to me a lot, like... well I guess like a big brother. With our Dad gone, I'm it. But I'm nothing like my father and haven't given Joey much time lately.

I'm doing my best to keep my party life and friends away from him and my Mom.

I live a double life lately; I get high and I've been lying. Getting stoned is so far from my Mom's mind that she wouldn't even know what to look for. I walk into the living room and see Uncle Lou helping Trisha with a crossword puzzle.

He turns to me. "Hey here's the scholar. I see you're helping your Mom out. Good man."

"Yeah, hey, Uncle Lou thanks for coming."

"You know, I think she's becoming a better cook than your grandma. She's open to doing some new things you know."

"Oh, really. I can't wait to tell Gram what you think."

"You do and you're dead!" he warns me.

My grandmother settled out by her sisters on Long Island. She sent a card with cash and called last night to wish me well. Other than that, we haven't talked much in months. I've been too busy to write or call.

My Dad's mom lives with his sister Carmela in Naples, Florida. The ocean is in her blood. She can cook octopus so tender you can cut it with a fork. One way she'd prepare it was as 'pulpo carpaccio,' as she called it. She'd slowly cook the octopus in its own liquid with bay and spices and then chill it in a loaf pan under a heavy weight in the fridge. She'd then let it set, congealing overnight in its own gelatin. She'd slice it paper-thin and serve it over arugula drizzled with olive oil, a squeeze of fresh lemon, parsley and capers…

Uncle Lou's voice snaps me out of my daydream.

"Did Carmela ever teach you how to make her zeppoles acci-ughe?" Uncle Lou asks.

"Yeah man, and I'll never tell," I say. She'd make the lightest zeppoles with anchovies. She brought fried dough to a new level. She'd sprinkle grated lemon and chives into the dough before she'd fold in the anchovy. After frying it she'd roll it in parmesan, fresh black pepper.

"I miss Christmas with your Dad's family ever since they moved to Florida," he says. "I remember she'd serve a pile of smelts lightly fried. Perfect."

There was an art to her frying. Clean oil, right temperature, drain properly, and never really heavy coatings on things. She didn't fry much, a couple of times a year, but when she did she'd be sure to use the oil wisely; she never wasted a thing. She'd pour the oil through a cheesecloth and use it again for the fried calamari and baccala.

Food was the drug passed around at my Grandmother's. She was the pusher and gave us the goods for free. "Why you no visit more?" I'd hear in broken English. Leaving me a guilt trip as the cost.

No one left the table with empty stomachs, ever. And all left with a stash of calories that could carry us for two weeks without eating. But it would only be the very next day you craved more of what only she can deliver.

Never much alcohol around the table or in the house though, just some wine, homemade limoncello, and brandied cherries. My father would drizzle Sambuca over his vanilla ice cream.

Uncle Lou speaks up, putting a stop to my wandering mind.

"Hey Nick, come check out Trisha blowing through this puzzle here. It's the Manhattan skyline from above. She just started it yesterday and she's almost halfway through it."

I look over the picture on the box cover and see an aerial shot looking down over the whole island of Manhattan, skyscrapers, and cathedrals; all seem to be from a bird's eye view.

"I don't know how you do it, Trish, but that's pretty amazing," I say.

She doesn't say a word and just keeps concentrating. I hear the screen door slam shut in the kitchen.

"Now go change your clothes and wash up before dinner. You're filthy," my mom's voice rises above the sounds of her prep work.

"Yeah okay Ma, but you won't believe what I just did on the bike," my brother answers.

"You're outside for twenty minutes and it's like you took a bath in mud. I don't know why every kid has to have a dirt bike up here. We were fine with bicycles in the city."

"It was sooo cool, Ma. One day, you should come down to the track and I'll show you."

"Sooo cool huh, like Fonzie? Well I'm not going down to that sand pit any time soon, honey. The noise down there is deafening.

You just be careful, wear your helmet, and you better not be riding alone. Now go upstairs, wash up, and come right down. I need you to make the meatballs for the soup."

Within a minute my little brother comes walking into the living room.

"Hey Pigpen, what's happening?" Uncle Lou says.

"I'm popping wheelies now Unc," he answers.

"What the hell is that? You think you're Evel Knievel or sumptin'?" Uncle Lou says.

"A wheelie, huh...you popping wheelies?" I ask. "Pretty cool. Now go wash up, cuz we're gonna eat."

"Hey, where's Gina?" Joey asks.

They all love Gina; she's like family. She's been around the house since they can remember.

"She's home, you little flirt. I'm meeting up with her later at Lisa's party."

"You guys should come check out my jumps and wheelies. I could ride one for a long time now," he says excitedly.

I put my arm around him and pull him close and rub his head.

"Yeah, I tell you what. Gina and I will come down and take some pictures. Then you could show them to mom," I say. "Now go change."

I give him a little nudge.

I was glad when my cousins and uncle all left that night. I kinda wanted to get to the real party that I'm sure has already started at Lisa's. And I really could have used a beer during dinner, but I'm just not there yet with Mom at the table, even though I'm of age.

Joey's helping her with the dishes and Trisha heads back to the living room to work on her jigsaw puzzle. I go to my room to change for the party, but first I open my bedroom window and put a box fan in it, and lower the window back down to secure it. I turn it on, so it pulls the air from the room, blowing out. I get out my small bong and the bag of weed that's hidden in the back of my closet.

I pack the tiny one-hit bowl with pot and put a lighter up to it. And with one long slow inhale I burn the weed into glowing embers as I listen to the bubbling bong water. As soon as I lift my finger off the hole in the back of the bong, a blast of smoke shotguns into my lungs.

I quickly grab a towel that's over the chair and start coughing like hell into it, trying to silence myself. Thankfully, I'm on the second floor and the kitchen is downstairs.

I'm a little dizzy from coughing, but it passes, and I calm down. I figure I'll pack another hit knowing my mom and Joey are downstairs busy with the dishes. I light it, and the coughing is less this time. I exhale out through the fan.

I look around at my room, which is a big mess. *I've really got to clean this place up*, I think to myself. Then my body starts to relax as the effect of the weed takes hold, and spreads to my head and limbs like fluid. I quickly scratch the thought of straightening up my room.

When I started having too many things to hide from my mom. Like pot, paraphernalia and Playboys, I asked her not to help in my room. A couple of years back.

I'll pick up some stuff off the floor, throw out my garbage, and give her my dirty laundry. But I rarely do more than that. I can't remember the last time I made my bed. It doesn't seem to make sense just to mess it up again the next night. Between school, work, and partying, lately, I've just been coming home to sleep, shower, and change anyway.

I think of Gina and can't wait to see her tonight. We've been going steady since we were fifteen, but we met when we were six. Running after fireflies and frogs led to holding hands and hide and seek. Then it was awkward French kissing and rolling around in the grass by the pond. By the middle of our junior year, the innocence and puppy love stopped, the condoms came out and we were now committed to each other. Doing it every chance we could get.

I wash up in the bathroom and splash on Brut aftershave, blast Binaca in my mouth, and drop in some Visine to clear any red out of my eyes. I'm all ready for Lisa's pool party tonight except for one more thing. I reach into the back of my bureau and peel two squares off a row of Trojans and slip them into my back pocket. Something's blocking the drawer from shutting, it's full of stuff, and I see a big book is in the way. It's taking up a lot of space and I can't even remember the last time I read a book. I pull it out; it's the Bible I got for my confirmation. I throw it in the trash to get a head start on cleaning out my drawers. I'm not about to read it, don't believe that stuff anymore. I'm not sure I ever did anyway.

I walk into the living room and I suddenly hear "Let It Be" playing again and it annoys the hell out of me for some reason. I look over to my sister Trisha.

"Hey, Ma. Why does Trisha have to play that same song over and over again? It drives me nuts, how can you take it?" I ask.

Every time I'm home, it's on. I've already heard it eight times since I've been home today. But it's probably the 25th time today for my mother. I look over at Trisha and she's looking over her puzzle as usual, always with a smile.

"Hey, she really likes it," my mom says. "She can hear you know. Why don't you just ask her?"

"No wonder someone shot that guy," I snap. "The sixties are so played out."

Trisha's blue eyes narrow, inspecting me sternly. Her expression changes to deep concern, assessing, as if she sees something strange about me, like she knows something. She knows I'm stoned I think.

31

Oh, man, I feel paranoid, and I'm getting cotton mouth. She can't know I'm high, I assure myself.

"Nick that's awful. Why would you say that?" mom questions, with a perplexed look. "That was very tragic – some demented fan thinks he's talking with 'little people', demons.

And by the way, Paul McCartney sang this song."

I roll my eyes. "Yeah, okay. Sure, Ma...demons, right. McCartney, Lennon, whoever, that music's played out. Love me do, wanna hold your hand, blah, blah."

"Nicholas, what's up with you?" my mom says.

"Nothing, Ma. I'm just tired of hearing that song over and over again."

"Nicky you behave. You're not being nice," Trisha's wearing her favorite blue dress with the lace collar again. Reminds me of her condition, how repetitive she can be.

I bend down a little, and kiss the top of her head. She's getting taller, thinning out. Her glasses keep getting thicker.

"Oh Sis, I'm sorry. If you like it, and it works for you, then fine. But right now, I'm outta here, okay?" She looks up at me with bright troubled eyes magnified by the lens.

"You...you...behave Nicky." Her finger pointing at me, like a little old lady.

"Whoa...okay Sis."

"You have fun, drive safe! And, NO drinking!" Mom adds bittersweet instructions.

"Yeah. OK. Sure, Ma. What do you mean? I'm eighteen, I'm legal."

"Not on that death trap! You better not be boozing and driving, or I'll run you over myself."

"I'll be fine Ma. See you later..."

"And we'll talk about that earring another day," she adds. No one else noticed.

Heading to the door I see Trisha get up from the puzzle and goes to leave the room. I round the corner to the front door, and hear my mom.

"Hey Trisha, where are you going sweetheart?"

"I…I… need to pray for Nicky, he needs help." I stop short of the door.

"Oh, well… okay honey, don't be long, we're having tea and another slice of the ricotta cheesecake with honey. Remember?"

Trisha just repeats herself, her voice fading as she leaves the room.

I laugh under my breath. She prays all the time; says she talks to Angels. But she rarely skips dessert, and never her favorite. *Humph…*

I grab my helmet and head out the door.

Chapter Three

Teenage Wasteland

"I don't need to be forgiven…"

~ The Who

I PASS A FLUTTERING CLUSTER of moths around the porch light as I pull my helmet on, swing my leg over the taillight, and straddle my bike. The night's breeze is a welcome relief from today's scorching heat. My helmet can't drown out the unceasing sound of crickets. I turn my key illuminating the green and red lights around my gauges. I bought this motorcycle pretty cheap from a guy whose girlfriend just had a baby, and said he needs a car now to get them around. When I saw it in the want ads, an all-black and chrome Yamaha 750, their 'Midnight Special', I realized it was just what I wanted.

Some guys have crotch rockets, cafe racers; they're all about speed. But I couldn't see cruising with Gina on the back of one of those a couple of years ago when I got this. I usually skip the electric start because one kick always starts it right up. I rev it a bit and settle into the seat. I buckle my helmet, the rumble and vibration of the motorcycle never fails to excite me.

There're two routes to Lisa's I can take – either King's Highway, which is a pretty straight route, but narrow and boring, or Snake Hill Road, which is a dimly lit, winding road that eventually heads up to Bald Mountain along the New Jersey border. It's a fun ride past the swamps and quarry. I just need to keep an eye out for the potholes.

I turn onto Snake Hill Road. The chrome of a truck's radiator grill quickly appears from the curve up ahead. I shudder with the sudden thought of my Dad's death. Its headlights blind me momentarily. The hood is so close I can see the chrome bulldog ornament clearly, as it reflects a mysterious red glow that pulses brighter – someone's brake lights I'm guessing.

The force of wind from the truck's wake sways my bike. My knees instinctively squeeze the fuel tank between my legs. A thrilling rush flows through me. *I got this.* I take a firm grip on the handlebars and then accelerate. I'm in total control. Several pairs of headlights from behind the truck whizz by. Each vehicle's draft that tugs on my bike gives a bit of a thrill.

There's no traffic in sight, as an opossum runs across the road, startling me. Summer bugs smack my face shield and a deer appears out of the woods on the side of the road.

In the beam of my headlight, a large mangy dog stands on the road just ahead – a viscous-looking wolf-sized hound. It looks sick with rabies or something. Its eyes are mad and a piercing red. It stands right in my path, not budging, looking directly at me. Very freaky, I think.

I instinctively cut the bike to avoid hitting it. The sudden move steers me quickly off the road, causing the bike to jump the curb, and I lose balance as the bike goes airborne. I quickly push it away from me and fall hard. My helmet bouncing off the curb and my body hard off the ground knocking whatever breath in me right out. My body feels immobile as I slide down the wooded embankment following my bike over gravel, leaves, and grass towards the edge of the marsh. I wheeze for a breath of air as the bike comes to a sudden stop, wedging itself under a large fallen tree, still idling. My front wheel's twisted with the headlight shining up into the trees above the road.

I've heard of having the wind knocked out of you... well now I know. I manage a moan and I'm able to catch a strained breath. Unable to move a thing, I just lie there focused on the rise and fall of my chest. I'm glad I freed myself from the bike before it hit. You don't want to be under one when it goes down.

I didn't know my ears were ringing until they stopped. My breath becomes steadier and I manage to pull my helmet off. I hear the crickets. I feel exhausted without doing a thing. I've dropped bikes before, and I'm glad to realize that I have no serious injury.

I'm stranded and not sure what shape the bike is in yet, which really sucks. The area is such a creepy place, marshy with rotten trees, mud and moss. A steamy fog over the swamp seems to hover extending deep into the woods.

I think of Trisha and how she just said she needs to pray for me, and it's a bit freaky. Troubling. I picture her on her knees by her bed, head down and hands folded in prayer, like I've seen her at times through the years. She'd speak of the luminous orbs that hover above her. And how these Angels would carry her prayers to God. And all I can think of is, *thanks Trish*, for all these blessings and good fortune. But please stop praying, it just doesn't work. There's no Angels or God. Not by looking at this mess. Or how my Dad died, so tragically, right in front of us.

I lay in pain and frustration at the bottom of the embankment then struggle to get up. I can see car headlights flash by up over the edge of the road. They have no clue I'm down here.

Leaves rustle and a twig breaks behind me. I look and suddenly see that mad dog through the mist of the bog, moving towards me. The hairs stand on the back of my neck. Oh, great, this wild dog is checking me out.

As I look around for a rock or a stick, I hear the rumble of a Harley. My headlight still cuts through the trees into the night sky over the road. As the roar approaches, I realize there's more than one. I see a sudden burst of light up on the road near where I wiped out. Then I hear muffled voices as a headlight beam turns from the road and drifts down into the bog, scanning the area. The light momentarily blinds me and I'm suddenly concerned about where this damn dog is.

I hear a man's voice.

"Hey there's a kid down here."

"Hey! Help! Help me man," I yell out loud.

My bike is stuck and I have no idea what condition it's in. It'll be hard as hell pushing it up the bank alone. And some pain is kicking in. I hear a different voice.

"I'm coming bro, we hear you, coming down." I struggle to pull the bike out, but the tree won't allow it.

"Hey I'm gonna need help man. My bike's stuck!"

I take off my helmet and toss it on the moss, glancing around for the dog but all I see are three rough-looking, burly bikers approaching me down the embankment.

One of them comes sidestepping down. "Hey kid…you all right, you hurt?"

The second one following suddenly stops. "Hey Mick, check that out."

I look over with the first biker and see the wild dog lurking beyond the steamy bog, it's form as black as a shadow as it enters into the brush along the edge of the swamp.

"Yeah that damn dog, that's why I wiped out. Really screwed me up," I say.

They both look over at the animal again, concerned. "So I see." one says.

"You think it's got rabies man?" I ask.

"Rabies? Nah, it looks like it's been fed, but hungry for more. Just like a dog, huh."

The third biker is already working on getting the tree off the bike.

"Hey Gabe, gimme a hand lifting this tree would ya?"

"You don't want to deal with this dog trust me, there's no satisfying it," Mick says.

"Yeah, coming Ralph, just a sec." Gabe says.

He stares straight at the hound and its red eyes radiate back through the bush looking right at him. He doesn't say a word and just faces off with it and the mangy dog suddenly snarls, turns, and takes off. This dude must know dogs or something.

"What's with his red eyes man…sick," I say.

"I know, weird right. What's your name kid?" He asks.

"Nick"

"I'm Gabe, this here is Ralph, and that's Mickey," he says.

"Nick looks like you're having a rough ride. In a bit of a pickle bro?" He adds.

"C'mon man, no kidding, wiped out and my bike's stuck."

"Yeah well, that's the easy bit, my man," he says.

Mickey and Ralph pick the tree up and move the motorcycle. Mickey picks my bike up, and then straddles the front wheel while holding the handlebars looking over its alignment. Ralph carefully walks around me, looking me over, and then picks up my helmet.

"I don't see blood. Anything feel broken kid?"

"No." He brushes my helmet with his hand then hands it to me.

"How's your head. This thing took quite a hit."

I've got a cramp in my neck and my shoulder aches a bit, but my head feels okay.

"No. No, man I'm cool. Just knocked the wind out of me."

Mickey singlehandedly pushes the bike up the embankment like it's nothing.

"Bike's fine. Just a few scratches and mud."

I'm shaking still, happened so fast, never had the wind knocked out of me before. I dust myself off as I trek up to the road. My bike looks okay. I start it up, and it sounds fine. I rev it a little and check my lights. The bikers return to their motorcycles and put on their helmets.

I take a deep breath as I hold my bike and breathe a sigh of relief.

"Thanks, you guys. No, like, thanks A LOT. You guys wanna smoke a joint?"

"No bro, don't smoke. Makes me choke. Just hang in there. You're lucky my friend here caught sight of the light." Gabe says.

"What light?" I ask.

"Your headlight was shining over the road up into the trees," he says.

"Oh yeah, right, lucky I guess."

"Don't believe in luck brother, someone up there must like you," Ralph says.

Mickey cuts in and asks: "Nick, right?"

"Yeah"

"Just slow down...and stay on the path my man. Seen enough kids check out too soon."

"Will do guys. Man, I can't believe it… thanks again."

I see the name on their leathers. "The Messengers" the patch reads. Never heard of them. And we have our share of bikers passing through to upstate New York all the time in the summer.

They mount their bikes. And I see them take off toward the fork in the road and bear right up the high road towards the full moon and they disappear around a bend. The light of the moon illuminates the mountain road clearly.

Brushing myself off, I see my jeans caught grass stains. As I wipe dirt off the chrome with a rag from under my seat, I take a good look over my bike. I pick up a stick and scrape away the soil and grass that's packed into my foot rest. I'm feeling lucky as I run the rag over the deep gravel scratches on my helmet. Happy it wasn't my head. I kick start my bike and shift gears towards the fork in the road ahead. Either route will get me to Lisa's party. I bear left, down the low road; it's darker but the more common route.

I pull up to Lisa's street and there're cars parked up and down both sides. I drive up Lisa's driveway and park on the lawn. Several girls I know from school are crossing the front lawn heading towards the rear of the house. I follow them to the backyard into the party. I immediately hear a voice call out "Nickeee," then another loudly "Yo Nick, over here". Sounds like Pauly, I head towards the voices. People acknowledge me in passing, and I stop a moment just to scan the whole scene. There's got to be over a hundred kids in every sort of rare form, partying. Although the yard is not very well lit, from the glow of the pool lights I can see a lot of familiar faces. Seeing many of the girls, for the first time, in bikinis. Cool.

Colorful Chinese paper lantern lights stretch from tree to tree on the outskirts by the grass. Webbed aluminum lounge chairs are all occupied, some with kissing couples around the patio. There are people sitting on the back lawn passing red glowing joints and bottles of liquor. A few couples in the shadows by the hedges are on blankets making out. A huge crowd is gathered over by the shed holding red cups. Keg. In the back corner by the fence some poor girl is wrenching, puking. Her friend holds her long hair safely away from her mouth. People are dancing, diving, wrestling, passing bongs, and Frisbee's. I'm psyched.

Large speakers are blasting "The Who's" *Who's Next* album and I'm feeling it.

The mellow start to their song "Getting in Tune" sinks into my ears deep. And I'm feeling in tune with it. A beer is all I need right now.

Lisa, our pretty hostess this evening, walks over to me with her younger sister Dana. They're both close friends of Gina.

"Hi ya Nick. Where's your beer?" Lisa asks.

"That's what I was just thinking."

"Kegs by the shed."

"That's what I figured. This party is cranking."

"Crazier than I thought. Hot night. Everyone's in the pool, hey, did you bring shorts?"

"Pool looks cool, all lit up like that." *Never saw lights in a pool before."* I didn't plan on swimming tonight, but I'm wearing designer underwear if that's okay to swim in?"

With pressure from Gina, I broke down and bought new colored underwear they're pushing, blue. There's no way she'll get me into the designer jeans she wants me to try on. That ain't happening. I wear Levi's.

A few bellbottoms, platform shoes, and a suede-fringed jacket are sitting back in the early 70's section of my closet. They won't be coming out again.

"Designer underwear...Are you really? Like Calvin Klein's?" she asks.

"Yeah, haha, surrre very cool. Let me see," she says between laughter.

"Five bucks."

"Ya know Chaz and you would make cute swimming buddies. He's wearing his blue Speedos."

"Funny, Ha. Ha. Hey where's Gina, have you seen her?" I ask.

"Yeah, she's around here somewhere, I think she's over by the pool. Hey, can you do me a huge favor and check on the grill, pleee-ase? Marcos is… like, so lost."

"Yeah sure, no problem." I say.

"There's plenty of burgers and stuff in the garage refrigerator if you need. Thanks, Nick!"

I notice Patsy walking up to me. His hair is getting longer, like hippie scrappy long. I've been buying weed from him ever since freshman year in high school. He used to sell loose joints for a buck or a nickel bag of pot for five bucks. His inventory has increased quite a bit, being the middleman for his older brother, Quinn, who lives in Hell's Kitchen in Manhattan. He supplies a stream of drugs from the city to the suburbs. He didn't graduate, but he's still in the circle of friends, always with the goods.

Patsy approaches me with a lit joint in hand and extends it out to me. Pauly is following behind him like a puppy, ready to party.

"Wuddup Nick? Prime doobage bro. Chamber weed. Had it in my pipe stem for like ten days" Patsy says to me.

Pauly steps right up excitedly. "I'm in."

I could use a good buzz, so I take this big hit. And I cough, hard... real hard. And I think, what am I like a wimp or something? I've taken big hits before.

"Told you dude. Its resin weed." Patsy's laughing at me. "Take smaller tokes bro."

Pauly cuts in after I'm coughing my brains out and taps my shoulder.

"Hey, pass it over... don't bogart that bone bro."

"Here, take it away man, knock yourself out."

Our friend Teddy walks up and steps right between Patsy and me and hands me a beer.

"Hey, thanks Teddy...man just what I needed." I immediately start cooling my throat with the suds.

"No problem bro. Got another two kegs on hold at the beer store." He loves beer and can probably out-drink anyone here.

Teddy's pretty straight, but he's a bit nuts. He's from a military family that moved around a lot when he was younger. Calling in a bomb-scare then blowing up M-80's in his locker freshman year got him expelled from Saint Augustine's High School. Now he says he wants to get into the NYPD.

"Two more kegs? So, I guess we better drink up!" I raise my plastic cup up to Teddy.

"Hey, how's Tina doing?" His girlfriend was out sick from school alot last year, I hand the joint to Pauly.

"She's coping, on meds,family issues. Why the hell do you smoke that crap, Nick?"

Pauly cuts right in before taking a toke. "It's just weed Ted, it's not like acid or heroin, geez. Grass is great, all I need."

Teddy's face lights up, he's looking at my earring. *Here it comes.*

"What the hell…What's that? You wearing an earring… an earring dude?"

I'm still coughing a bit and I look away and at the ground.

"C'mon Teddy. Blow up any lockers lately?" *Why'd I just say that?*

"I think it's righteous, man. It's a statement. I'm thinking about it, you know, I just may get one," Patsy says. He should know better than to give Teddy his opinion by now.

Teddy puts his face in Patsy's, boot camp style and loudly says, "Shut up Patsy, you drop-out pusher punk. Who cares! Go smoke another joint."

Patsy just takes it in stride. He knows Teddy's not out to hit him. Teddy just hates him.

I look straight over Teddy's shoulder and I see Marcos covered in smoke, with flames flaring high on the grill in front of him.

I cut in. "Oh, man. Hey guys... Marcos, I gotta go give him a hand."

They turn and look over at Marcos and start cracking up at the scene. He's in an apron waving a spatula into the smoke, jumping up and down a bit, and burning himself as he tries to reach things on the grill, but the flames are too intense.

I quickly head over there passing through people, tiki torches, and lawn furniture.

Marcos has been all through junior high and high school with us.

46

He's a tall, thin, brown kid who's very proud that he has the biggest afro. There isn't much competition in this neighborhood. His hair always has a black afro pick sticking out of the back of it. Amazingly, he can eat more than three of us put together without gaining an ounce. Nobody's sure if it's his metabolism or a tapeworm. He actually hits the gym to gain weight.

He never met his parents or knows what race he is. No one knows. He tells me the Sisters at St. Francis named him Marcos 'cos he looked Puerto Rican. The story goes that he was left a newborn on the steps of their chapel wrapped in a towel in a plastic milk crate back in the Bronx.

He's fortunate to have been raised by the Sisters in the suburbs. No one adopted him. He thinks it's because his right eye is cockeyed. He's out of the boys' home and on his own now that he's eighteen.

"Hey smoky! I know black is beautiful, but not on the chicken, Bro!" I reach out and nudge him away from the grill and he willingly hands over his spatula. "You better watch that 'fro don't go up in flames, my man."

His eyes are watering as he waves the smoke away from his face.

"Man oh man, geez... Nick! Thank God. Gimme a hand, would ya?"

The burgers and chicken are in flames because they're too close together dripping grease. I start tossing burnt items into the trash.

I put what's salvageable around the perimeter where it's a lot cooler allowing it to become nearly smokeless, organized, and cooking fine.

Marcos wipes his eyes with the red bandana from around his neck.

"Man, quick fix! Thanks, you da man." Marcos says.

"No problem, dude. Hey, I think you need a brew. Me too, wanna go grab a couple?"

Marcos is composing himself by jabbing the pick through his 'fro.

47

"Yeah sure, oh chef-of-the-future. Grilling sure as hell ain't easy."

"My Dad taught me a few things."

Grilling was the job for the man of the house, and my Dad was really good at it. He'd do some amazing stuff on an open fire when we used to camp.

"Be right back. We'll blow a bone and you can show me." Marcos heads towards the keg.

"Okay sure," I say.

The long BBQ fork works perfectly to reach under the grill grate and even out some of the coals. I lift the lid off the large cooler on the ground next to the grill, poke around and pull out a package of thick brown deli paper. It contains a beautiful coil of sweet sausage. I flip it onto the grill and toss out the wrapping into the trash can behind me.

It begins to sizzle and sear – that's gonna be delicious. It's very fresh and I can see the cheese and parsley throughout it. I look up through thin lines of smoke and see Gina through the dreamy heat wave that's radiating off the grill. Her bright broad smile and deep chestnut eyes are always honest, warm, and refreshing. Her long golden brown curls spring off her bare shoulders as she steps towards me.

Gina doesn't know how pretty she is, really. She never wears make-up, no need. An Italian-American "Ivory Soap" girl, "99% pure" like the commercial says. Her sweet disposition and love for life is contagious. I don't know what it is but people are drawn to her. She likes to help people, goes to church, and volunteers for stuff constantly, go figure.

My mom, brother, and sister all adore her. She enjoysspending time with Trisha so much it's amazing. She has alot more patience than I have with her, for sure.

Gina looks good in anything she wears, seriously. I think she's no doubt, model material. I'm always thrilled to see her and that's like every day.

Tonight, she's wearing her new, skin-tight Jordache jeans with a red and white striped tube top. She's baring her shoulders and belly for a change. More skin than usual. She still wears one-piece bathing suits.

"Hey graduate…congratulations!" I reach out to her.

"I know. Can you believe it? After all these years, FINALLY! Ear looks good," she says.

"Thanks, catchin' some serious flak about it." As we hug, I lean back and lift her off her feet and twirl her around a couple of times ending with a kiss on the lips, I step back over to the grill and quickly resume tending to it with one hand. I slip my other snugly into her back pocket.

"Hey, you doing okay? It was a big day today, you should be proud." She slides her arm around my waist and squeezes.

"Yeah… I wish he was there, ya know, 'big day', like you said." Carefully flipping the coil of sausage, I zone out, gazing at the glowing coals.

"I know your Dad was real proud today," she says with certainty.

"C'mon Gina…How do you know?" eyes still focused on the grill.

"I just do. Just because you can't see him, doesn't mean he's not there." She squeezes my waist again.

"Yeah when I see him, I'll believe it."

"It works the other way around. Believe then you'll see."

"Yeah, yeah. Okay Gina please not now." She slaps my ass.

"Okay…well you better not be on that grill all night, or I'll cook your butt!"

I arrange grilled items on a platter, and Gina places them on the buffet. People approach, grab food and a line forms. We're side by side filling the platters as people help themselves. I really enjoy doing this. Serving, she does too; a really promising partnership for our business venture.

"Isn't it wild how Lisa's pool lights up from the inside?" Gina asks.

"Yeah I know, right. Pretty awesome."

"We'll need that for night swimming at the spa. It's so cool looking."

"Yeah. Not sure how they put electric under water,"

"Oh. Oh, Nick I have to tell you. I saw a spa ad in Vogue and guess what? They have a menu for their services. They actually call it a 'menu'!"

"A 'menu' for haircuts? That's crazy."

"There's facials, pedicures, manicures all sorts of massages, and stuff. I cut out the article for us, I think it's a great idea." She's so excited.

"A menu huh? I guess we'll both be writing menus then…pretty funny. Hey, what do you think of pool tables and pinball machines?"

"No! The places I read about are nice and quiet, with yoga and stuff."

"Yoga, what's that? No yogurt or religion stuff," I say.

"It's not religion, it's a way to exercise and meditate."

"Okay, I guess. How about shuffle board or Bocce ball?"

"Maybe Bocce ball," she agrees.

"I know… a movie room! You know, wheel in a projector like in school. Everyone loves movies," I say.

"YES. Yeah…great idea. We'll show musicals and comedies. Feel good stuff at night." She says.

"I'm writing that down, that's cool, an in-house movie theatre… with cocktails and hors d'oeuvres." I look for a pen and paper to no avail.

Lisa's miniature collie approaches wagging his tail, Gina smiles wide. She loves all animals.

"And I want a sweet dog like Lisa's, but bigger, maybe two. And we'll grow our own flowers and vegetables in beautiful gardens," she says.

I take a knee on the bluestone patio to greet the happy pup, petting his head.

"Atta boy Buddy, how ya doing? Atta boy...good boy... It's Buddy, right Gina?"

Gina kneels down beside me and hugs him. He starts licking her face.

"Yeah. Heya Buddy, you are a good boy…yes, you are, okay, okay, 'nuff kisses."

Our friend Chaz approaches and we get up to greet him. I toss Buddy a cold hot dog, he turns and trots off with it in his mouth. Picking up some ice from the cooler, I rub it between my hands to rinse them. Chaz is a buff, blonde boy from L.A. He wears Speedos. But what's "in" at this suburban party is cut-off Levis. He gets away with it because he's on the swim team.

When he first came to our school he spoke like a spiffy surfer. Like a gnarly, tubular, bodacious, bogus dude. But this pretty boy from LA with his generous peace pipe of homegrown California bud quickly broke any East Coast, West Coast ice. He brought some weed from California that we only heard about. Acapulco Gold. It blew away the Jamaican dirt weed we were getting. It was everything we heard about. It was a beautiful golden color and kicked ass.

"Hey Gina…'sup Nick?"

Gina raises her hand up and high fives Chaz.

"Congrats Chaz!! Woo Hoo!" She's so excited. "I'll see you guys later. I have to find Lisa. She said she was gonna need a hand."

She kisses me on the cheek and heads towards the house.

"Okay, see ya later." I say.

"Later." Chaz says.

"Hey congrats on the diving scholarship, bro. You're booking back to LA I heard?"

"Yeah UCLA. Looks like that worked out... I'll be back living by my mom's. I'm set up with a place right off campus. Dude, I want you to come check it out!"

California? I've never given it a thought. Seems too far away.

"How long is the flight?" I ask.

"You're on the West Coast in five hours' dude. I take the flight all the time."

"Sure, man, I'd check it out. But I'm starting school upstate in September. Need to save my funds."

"A lot is happening with food in LA now dude. It's pretty health conscious, I hear. Peace, love, and granola. None of that stuffy French crap. It's just what you've been talking about. Spas and the whole bit."

He's right. I read about it in a food magazine I buy.

"The best fresh produce, avocados, sprouts, sushi, and seaweed," he continues on.

"I'd like to check it out, but friggin' grass sprouts? I tried them... taste like dirt. And the seaweed and raw fish, I don't know, not feeling that yet."

"It's Los Angeles man," Chaz says. "Mexican word, means "the Angels," you know like "Charlie's Angels, bro". The surf, the babes, killer bud, no snow tires, no gloves, no bugs, no rain, and no frigging helmets, I kid you not. My brother knows all the clubs now dude, he's bouncing a couple of places."

"No helmets? Man, I don't know about that one." I show him the stains on my jeans and jacket. "I ditched it on the way over, damn dog in the middle of the road, could've cracked my skull."

"You wiped out?" He checks out my jeans.

"Yeah, I slid out and my bike was stuck under a log dude, it was freaky. Some bikers stopped and helped me out. I scratched up my helmet good, could have been my face. But don't say nothing, okay dude. All's well. Just popped the curb," I say.

"Yeah, no problem. Not a word." He assures me.

"But no bugs, huh? Seriously? Cool."

"Hey, you gotta come out for spring break. All you need is your shorts and airfare, I got the space."

"No doubt! I'll check it out for a week or so, if the funds allow," I say. Our friend Phil comes sprinting towards us looking pretty uptight. Phil's anxiety is higher than most already and seeing him more uptight, well, I didn't know what we were in for. He doesn't drink beer, but pops speed and washes it down with a constant flow of Manhattan Special, an espresso soda packed with caffeine and sugar. I like him, but his instability puts me on edge sometimes.

"Hey, you guys... Jersey dudes are crashing the party." He stops and puts his hands on his knees, breathing heavily. "Val's old boyfriend from Park Ridge... there's like a bunch of jocks with him... scumbags."

I can't believe it. These guys should know better. We've had fights over the years in parking lots and carnivals, but to crash a party? It seems obvious they're looking to cause trouble.

"Park Ridge? Man, what are they trippin'?" I say.

"I'll book it to the backyard and get Teddy and some guys. We'll meet you in the front." Chaz says.

"Yeah, yeah okay…Cool. C'mon Phil, let's check it out," I say.

When we get around to entering Lisa's front yard, Phil and I notice across the lawn some Park Ridge guys leaning against their cars on the street. I scan the scene and see two guys talking to Lisa, Val, and Gina by the backyard gate. I recognize one guy, Ace, and he is getting real close as he talks to Gina. I've seen him before. He's well known and usually the troublemaker of the bunch.

He's 'scoping' Gina up and down, ogling over her tube top. And I swear he's got his hand in his pocket, playing in his underwear.

Phil and I cross from one side of the house, pass the front porch, and walk over to them near the back gate.

"I said like… ya know, like… it was cool for ya know… Robert to come, with a friend, not like, your whole football team." we hear Val say.

Lisa looks to Gina. "There are too many people back there now. My mom's gonna freak out!"

"It's not a good idea for you to stay. Ya know… it's too crowded. And it's just not cool." Gina says, as Lisa is getting visibly nervous.

We near them just as Ace reaches out and takes hold of Gina's forearm. He's leering at her tube top, grinning.

"You're plenty of reason to stick around here. Yes, good and plenty."

He stops playing pocket pool and takes his hand out to take hold of her other arm.

The fact that he just grabbed her arm is blowing my mind. Gina's pissed I can tell. I rarely see her mad, never in fact. There is no way this guy is getting out alive if he doesn't leave now. I have no fear of muscle heads or fights for that matter. And I'm lining up how I'm gonna hit this guy if I have to. My father taught me a few things about defending myself. Various street fights come every so often and I can stand my ground. But nobody's messed with Gina before and my blood is pumping. I step right into his space, steaming.

"Knock it off creep, let go of her," I say.

Phil repeats. "Yeah knock it off!"

Gina's suddenly pulls her arm away from him dropping her beer. She takes a sudden step back, crossing her arms over her chest, and looks away from Ace.

"Hey, relax sugar. Chill. I'll go get you another one. So, where's the keg?" He says.

"Get the hell outta here," I say.

Gina's avoiding eye contact with him. "Cut it out. You guys should really leave.," she says.

"Yeah I think that's the best idea." I walk up into his face.

"Hey, we just want to party man. No problems, I swear," Ace says.

Val's ex, Robert, cuts in. "Yeah, Val invited us."

"Like I said I invited you. No one else, ya know," Val says.

"So, Robert, you can stay," I say. "Everyone else can split."

"Well if he stays, I stay. If I stay, they all stay," Ace tells me as he looks over at the gang of Jersey guys by their cars.

I understand their dilemma. If one or two stay then there's a good chance that after having a few, someone here will pick a fight with the "Jersey dude," And there's no chance he'll win because it wouldn't be long before it'd no longer be a one-on-one fight.

Phil cuts in. "Oh yeah. And if they stay, you're really knee deep, and you'll all get your asses kicked."

Ace steps towards me. He's larger and may look tough but I don't care. A big pimply jock. Probably on steroids, I hear they all are lately.

He glances over at Gina again.

"I don't think so, I gotta get this little lady another brew."

I can't believe this guy. Rage builds up in me and I feel it rushing, burning its way up to my head. I step forward.

"Get outta here man, and go cop your own beer."

Ace leers at Gina again. "No...no, I like it here. I think we'll stay." He says calmly, assuredly.

"Cut it out. You guys better go... Go away please! It's too crowded," she says in a strained high voice.

Ace turns his head towards his friends and they begin approaching. He suddenly pushes me, causing me to take a step backwards. I step back into him, and I push him back much harder. He comes at me again.

"You're just a sissy hippie, with a fag earring," he says.

Phil steps up and reaches into his waistband. I can't believe he brought his gun to a pool party. "Cool it Phil, I got this. He's just a juiced-up goon."

I start taking my jacket off to free up my arms, but as soon as I drop the jacket behind my back and slide the sleeves down my arms, I'm suddenly caught in the tight bands on the end of my sleeves. Before I know it, Ace steps in and punches me twice in the face. I'm knocked back a couple of steps, and feel the sting in my eye.

Gina's several yards to my left, with her hands on her head shouting, "Stop it, stop it now. PLEASE!

Ace swings at me again and I dodge it. I'm hopping around, pulling on my sleeves trying to get this jacket off.

Teddy, Patsy, Pauly, and about fifteen guys from around back come jogging into the front yard. Some are carrying lawn darts.

Park Ridge guys approach Ace and me, and I see Central Valley guys start to form a circle around them.

Someone from the Jersey gang screams out. "Pop him again Ace!"

I hear another voice shout from the Jersey side. "Kick his ass!"

Ace nails me in the gut and sends me back several feet and comes charging towards me like he's gonna tackle me. I have no more time to struggle with the jacket. I focus on his face and see a perfect opportunity – I step toward him and swiftly bring my foot up under his chin, just like I'm punting a football.

"Yeah! Nick! Get him, Get him!" I hear from Pauly, I think.

The kick lifts him upright, stopping him short. His arms flail out by his sides and he stumbles back a few steps... He's down and out.

I turn around and there's fighting going on all around the yard.

Yelling, verbal threats, grunting, and growling, the usual and I know there's more to follow.

"Nick, watch your back!" Phil yells out.

I turn around quickly and swing my arms over my head with the jacket now in front and I end up wrapping it around an oncoming Jersey guy's head, strictly by accident. I push my knee hard into his back, and he stumbles to the ground tearing my jacket from my arms. I take a quick look and see Gina on the side of the yard standing alone. Where the hell are the girls? I wonder. I know she's concerned, worried, and not at all happy with what's going on. She doesn't understand all the fighting, wrestling, and stuff we're into.

All of us, whether it was with guys from Jersey or not, would end up wrestling, brawling with one another for one reason or another anyway, too much testosterone. For some of them, over the last few years, the night wasn't complete unless they got chased by the cops, hopped a few fences, hid from car headlights, and then laughed about it later. That's how we danced with each other in the suburbs – our Westside Story. Playing cat and mouse with Officer Krupke and fighting with the guys from across the tracks. The unwritten rule was no bats, no knives, and no weapons.

A scream pierces the air. Gina.

I look to the row of evergreens on the property edge where Gina was standing before. Ace is right up against her, forcing her into the bushes, holding a handful of her hair in his grip and controlling her head. I see that she's frantically pulling her tube top back up over her chest. He grabs her arm, pulling her closer towards him and I take off totally enraged.

I guess that kick wasn't enough. Now I want to kill him.

"Get the hell off of her!" I bellow.

He turns pushing her hard into the bushes and puts his fists up, but I have a running start and I tackle him full speed and begin pummeling him mercilessly.

I hear Teddy several minutes later yelling at me. It's like I blacked out.

"That's enough Nick. ENOUGH!" Ted and Marcos grab me and try pulling me off Ace.

Gina's yelling, "Nick STOP! STOP IT! PLEEAASE STOP!"

Both my arms are now gripped by Teddy and Marcos.

"He's out cold bro, lay off." Teddy yells.

"Dude calm down, man, calm down. You're scaring me bro, Gina's cool, she's okay now," Marcos says.

I look down at Ace and it looks like a wolf pack has let loose on him and he may just need a few stitches to say the least. I realize I'm breathing heavily and my hands are still shaking slightly.

Blacking out is a first. I didn't even realize he was unconscious.

The Jersey guys are outnumbered and take a beating. Marcos also takes a couple of hits trying to break a fight up, trying to keep the peace. Two Jersey dudes have Ace's arms around their shoulders as they carry him dragging his feet over to their cars.

They take off one by one, each trying to burn rubber loudly down the street, smashing beer bottles out the windows onto the road along the way. One car jumps the curb onto Lisa's lawn and tears it up, spinning its tires as it returns to the pavement screeching and smoking.

The whole party yells and curses them, before cheering their departure. They quickly disperse when two cop cars pull up in the front.

I pick up my jacket and step over to Gina, who's trembling. I wrap it around her and hold her close from behind then whisper in her ear.

"Don't worry...I'm here, I'm right here, everything will be all right."

The nervous quivering of her lips slowly relaxes, as she melts back into me.

Chapter Four

No Time

"Seasons change and so did I, you need not wonder why…"

~ The Guess Who

IF THE BOOZE, BEER, AND weed hadn't worn off from the night before, I probably wouldn't have felt my eye pulsing or the pain in my
ribs so much. But by mid-morning I have to get up and get some
aspirin. My head is aching, as I look at my eye in the dusty mirror
on my bureau. It's practically swollen shut: purple and blue and deep
red from a broken vessel or something. My first black eye and the
first time anyone's connected with my face in a fight. My Dad taught
me some boxing when I was a kid. He told me it was something he
picked up in the military. We jumped some rope together and hit
speed bags as well. He was always in top shape just like all of his
fireman buddies, or so I remember. I'm not sure how proud he'd be
of me if he saw Ace today though. I'm pretty sure he needed more
than a few stitches. But then again, it was for Gina.

My Dad loved Gina; she's been around us since grammar school,
like one of the family for over ten years. In fact, the day we made our
first communion was the day I asked her out. He was right there to
encourage me. We were only eight at the time.

I can feel it, like I'm reliving my eight-year-old self that very day.

I hope she can't tell that I'm trembling. My knees are weak and
my jaw feels locked. I'm nervous but thrilled that she took my hand
in hers first. I look to her, she smiles. Suddenly, I feel handsome.
Mom told me I was, nine times this morning. 'You're sooo…hand-
some'. I hear her voice assuring me in my head. The shakes stop and
I'm suddenly confident too in my brand new black suit. I begin sidestepping closer, inch-by-inch to her, my best friend, Gina Cinelli.
The cutest, coolest curly-haired girl ever, the one I have a serious
crush on since kindergarten. Can't believe we're actually holding

hands in front of the open church doors, me in my suit and her in her lacy white Communion dress. Silly, but I can easily imagine us just married. Blue sky and pure sunshine that's all around my Dad is welcome and warm, as he snaps pictures of us.

Gina's smile turns to a giggle, she cups her hand near my ear and whispers, "There's an angel on your shoulder." I turn my head to see, and she quickly steals a kiss on my cheek, it's warm, wet. My first. She giggles hysterically while squeezing my hand, hard.

I swiftly swipe my sleeve across my wet cheek. I can't contain the joy building inside, so it bursts out into a beam on my face. I feel it can last for days.

My mom, sister, and little brother pose next to us as Dad takes more photos.

I'm gonna ask her out. I signal my Dad; he leans down to me. I whisper in his ear so she can't hear.

"Hey Pop... can we take Gina to a movie? Maybe Willy Wonka and the Chocolate Factory?"

He listens intently. He always listens to me. Always cares about what's on my mind. I'm glad I can tell him anything.

"Sure, sure we can. A Saturday matinee, sounds good," he says with certainty and a smile.

I knew he'd say yes. I just had to ask him.

"You don't think it'll be like "Fantasia" was, do you?" I ask. Remember, that was rated G too, you know."

"Fantasia? Oh, boy. Still having bad dreams, Bud?" My head hangs low.

A terrifying scene of the devil and Hell towards the end of it frightens me so much that I have nightmares. I sometimes jolt out of bed and slip into theirs many nights because of it.

My Dad squeezes my shoulder again, pulling me closer.

"You're a big guy now." he says. I may be bigger, but I still get them. I just don't run to their bed anymore.

"So, are you going to treat? Be kind, spend some money?"

"Of course, the Cokes and popcorn too. Then can we stop at Dairy Queen? I'll use some Communion money from Uncle Lou for ice cream."

"Sounds excellent, and generous. Now the thing you need to do is ask her Dad if you can treat her to a movie. That's his little girl you know."

"*Her* Dad? No way! Can't you ask him Pop? He scares me."

"Scary or not, if you want to take her, then you'll have to have the courage to face him and ask his approval... her Dad's blessing."

"Man...seriously, Pop? Geez, Oh boy... all right."

He puts his arm around me squeezing me close again; this time he leans down and kisses the top of my head. "Good, 'cause that's what a gentleman does."

Intense pain in my ribcage brings me back to the current reality, my swollen face in the mirror. Also, confirming the sad truth, I'm older, not as innocent and my Dad is still gone. I open the medicine cabinet and take out a bottle of aspirin and pop three. I cup my hands under the running faucet and slurp tap water. I tilt my head back dripping liquid from my chin to my chest as I gulp down the pills.

It's hard to imagine I was ever really that small, young, and innocent. I mean, I was always looking to be older, thrilled when I got my pubic hairs at twelve. Then it was facial hair at fourteen, wishing I was sixteen to get a license. Then I couldn't wait for eighteen so I could get into bars. Now, I'm eighteen, and I like it.

Passing my fingers through my hair, I head to my room and pick up the bong. It's a morning ritual a few times a week, whenever I have weed. Opening my window to put the box fan in, I see my mom's car gone and remember she was going shopping with Trisha and Joey today. Cool, she's not gonna see my face and I don't have to explain it to Trisha and Joey. It is what it is, I'm glad I'm not that guy Ace that's for sure. I throw on shorts and a t-shirt and head down the steps to get the mail.

I open the mailbox and flip through the envelopes and there it is, the letter from the school. I anxiously open it. Even though the regimen and discipline of school turns me off, these last few years in the kitchens really excited me. I really want this. I know there's much more to explore. Many friends heading to college still aren't set on their majors, let alone if they'll even like what they choose. I'm actually one of the few who does.

Within seconds of opening the envelope I'm feeling sick to my stomach as I read "We regret to inform you due to …"

"No. NO! Damn!" I read to where it says I can re-apply and then stuff the letter in my shorts and shove the mail back in the box.

I put on my helmet, hop on my bike and take off aimlessly. I screwed up. I could kick myself.

The regret is short lived when I suddenly remember I read that the best chefs never even went to college. They learned by doing, working. Apprenticeships. Many top chefs in Europe never even finished high school. Plenty of my food magazines confirmed that. Why do I have to learn French cooking to be a chef in America anyway? I'm pretty sure Spain, China and Italy could care less what the French are cooking. Who said we have to?

I pull up in Chaz's driveway, hop off, and enter his backyard. He's springing off a diving board. When he gets out, he grabs a towel and walks over to me.

"Hey dude…OUCH! I see that chump connected before you kicked his ass," he says.

"Yeah well he's lucky he didn't play with me today. I probably would have killed him." I quickly flash the open letter. "Got this today, letter of rejection."

He shakes his head sadly. "Whoa dude... bummer. Fricking school don't know a good thing. That's their loss dude."

"Damn bro... I really wanted this. I thought it was in the bag."

"Yeah, but look what opened up." Chaz says, smiling wide. "You're gonna come to Los Angeles, aren't you? Ha Ha ha! I sold you on it last night, didn't I?"

I nod. A lot happening with food out there. Right?" I say feeling a bit numb.

"Yes! Yes. That's right! This is so cool bro. It's great, you'll see! An endless summer... you'll love it!"

Then reality sets in. "Yeah but... Gina's accepted to FIT in Manhattan. I want her to come."

"That's an issue. Look the place is small, but that's cool, till you two can find something.

"She has no idea, it just came to me. She's set on this school, I don't know what she'll say." I'm feeling anxious, eager almost, 'cos I know I'm going to do this.

Chaz gives me a *no sweat* wave with his hand towards me.

"She loves you man. She'd follow you anywhere. And there's a good fashion school right in LA she could get into. I bet my brother can hook you up in a kitchen too, he knows that whole LA circuit."

That's it, I'm set to go and feel like leaving tomorrow.

"I'm definitely going, and I'm counting on Gina too. I'll call you later for details."

I immediately start dreaming of California with Gina. For me, I know it's the answer. I'll get a job out there in a kitchen for the next couple of years, and learn what all the buzz is about from the inside. I'm sure Gina will be excited as I am.

I pull up to Gina's, shut the bike, and roll up the driveway quietly in neutral. I'm glad to see she's in her car 'cos I really didn't want to knock on the door with my eye like this. She's hanging her graduate tassel onto the rearview mirror. I slip into her car on the passenger side.

"G'morning Gina."

"Hey honey! Oooh…ow, wow your poor eye. That must really hurt."

I lean in and kiss her cheek. "The eye's fine." I look in the car mirror and say, "Don't even feel it." The aspirins are working cos' I don't feel my ribs either.

"Well it sure doesn't look fine. You should see a doctor. It's all bloodshot."

She takes a closer look and slowly runs her fingers through my hair. "I hate fights. I shudder just thinking about that guy last night."

"He was a chump. A steroid muscle-head." I say.

"And you're my hero…" She wraps both arms around my neck and kisses me.

I'm not sure how to say what I have to tell her, my sudden plan to move West is gonna throw her for a loop.

"Hey Gina, you know how I was late sending in that school application?

"Yeah, they said they'd review it. Right?

"Yeah well, they did. Damn it… I got the letter, I won't be going. I didn't get in."

She squeezes my hand tight. "Uh-oh… aww honey. Hey, so what? I'm sure you'll be in for next semester or, so, right?"

"I'm not going next semester or next year. I'm not reapplying."

"Don't say that. It couldn't hurt to get a few credits at the county college and then reapply next year."

"Well a better door opened up already, and it's not the county college. Hey, what do you say we go west to LA for a while?"

"LA? Why would you want to go there? And what do you mean 'we'?"

"Did you know... That the best chefs in the world never even finished school…"

"C'mon Nick, you can't be serious," she says looking right at me, almost laughing.

"No, I am serious. And why would we want to go to Los Angeles? Are you kidding me? There's gold there, baby... *Gold*! It's even called the Golden State. Plenty of sunshine, swimming pools, and beaches. The palm trees and parties." I take a quick breath, remembering Chaz's words hoping she catches my excitement. "Don't you want to see Hollywood and all the movie stars? We'll go to Disneyland and Malibu. And Chaz told me about all the yachts, hot tubs, and hot cars. Oh, and there's money. Lots of money like *Beverly Hillbillies* kind of money. There's no bugs or snow...just think about that."

"You're crazy. You never mentioned LA before," she says gently, shaking her head.

"I know, but there's a lot happening with food there the last few years. And don't forget all the pretty people who need beauticians. Like Farrah Fawcett, or, you know, Cheryl Tiegs. It'll definitely help us to tighten up the spa plan."

"Trust me, Farrah Fawcett has plenty of beauticians willing to work on her for nothing. C'mon Nick, be real. You know I'm going to school in the fall," she firmly says.

Gina's Dad is in the garden holding up a basket full of zucchini blossoms towards us.

"Hey, join us for breakfast?" he says waving from across the yard.

I'm glad he can't see the right side of my face. I wave back.

"Thanks Mr. Cinelli, but I really can't this morning." I belt out quickly. He acknowledges with thumb up and continues to pick blossoms.

I have no appetite, and there's no way I want them to see my eye swollen shut. But I do like squash blossoms for breakfast. He dips them in flour, then egg and sautés them in olive oil. He tops them with fresh ground pepper and grated parmesan. He also stuffs them with Fontina cheese and chives then breads and deep-fries them.

"I'll be in soon." Gina says outside the car window

She turns to me. "He wants to back us Nick. He really likes the idea."

"I know. But I'm thinking big Gina. I'm not talking pizzeria or Ma and Pa spa. He's talking everyday people, and I'm thinking real high-end, like in the magazines."

"Well it kinda was his idea, ya know," she says.

Her Dad told us of how his parents used to go to upstate NY in the summer to Saratoga or even further north to Sharon Springs for mineral baths. If it weren't for him, I never would have heard of a spa. People would get away and relax for a few days or a week and then go back to the city. Mineral baths were nothing new, but these places faded out when more people started flying everywhere. He spoke of reviving a small one and making it a year-round destination place to relax. I knew in my gut that learning to cook fresh and healthy, like the latest magazines I've been reading, was the right step.

"I really think we should do this. Go to Cali. We'll hook up with Chaz and stay with him near UCLA, till we get a place." Gina's anxiously playing with her hair, I think she's coming around.

"I'm open to it... but why don't you just go and check it out for a couple of weeks or something? It's a big decision. And who will we know besides Chaz anyway?" Not what I wanted to hear.

"We know each other Gina... we have each other. Just picture it... you and me on the beach, gazing into the sunset with a warm summer wind. And margaritas". She slowly shakes her head looking down to her lap. Her frown deflates my hopes.

"I can't Nick. It's so sudden. You know I'm starting school soon."

"Chaz says there's a great school for you right in LA."

"You really think my Mom and Dad would be okay with me changing schools and us living together? Trust me they wouldn't be thrilled."

"So, don't tell them. Or just tell them we're not." she looks at me surprised.

"Really Nick? You know that's a lie."

"Yeah I know."

"And what about our plans... you know first school, the spa business..." she asks.

"Yes, yes, of course, except the school part, for me, for now. It's still the plan. I'm just talking about the next couple of years." I suddenly realize I'm asking a lot of her, crossing a line. She doesn't like to lie and I'm disturbing her plans to accommodate the change in mine. But the next two years just opened wide for me and I really believe this move will benefit both of us.

Gina slowly raises her head and looks at me eye to eye. "Well what if things didn't quite happen in that order."

"Things are already out of order. I didn't expect this, but, like I said, the best chefs never went to school...and that's a fact. You know what? I'm cool with that."

Gina starts to fidget with the steering wheel, tracing it with her index finger, and says, "I mean more like...things out of order, you know, with us. We are sleeping together you know... we agreed not to wait."

"I wouldn't call it sleeping but...Wait? Nobody waits anymore," I say certainly.

"So, what if I got... ya know, pregnant? We would need family around for help, support."

"What? Oh pleeaase Gina...don't talk like that. We're careful. We're not stupid."

"But even then, surprises happen. You know I was okay with all the other cuddling and stuff. We didn't have to go all the way. We could've waited longer." My heart drops.

"Are you pregnant?" My eye throbs, my ribs ache, and my mind's being blown.

"I know we hardly discussed if that happened, but relax, I'm just a couple of days late."

My heart starts pumping faster it seems.

"Whoa! Geez Gina...if you're pregnant, we'll have to... well, we'll have to…"

"Yeah, yeah - have to what?" She asks calmly.

"Well, you know... take care of it." I say.

She smiles. "I know, I know, of course. But it won't be easy without family and on our own."

I turn my focus to a stain on the carmat. "I meant an abortion." I break gently.

Gina gasps, startling me. She covers her mouth.

"That's "taking care" of it? Oh, my God, Nicholas... how can you even say that?" She turns her face away to the window, slowly shaking her head.

"Teddy's girlfriend, Rachel, got one a couple of years ago. You're in and out, they won't even tell your mom." I try saying calmly, but fail being extremely anxious.

"I know all about Rachel. She's still in therapy, and her parents have no idea that it may be the reason…and it is." she says with moist eyes quickly turning back to the window.

"Gina, are you really pregnant or not?"

She shakes her head and assures me. "No... No ...I'm not. I told you that!" She's now shaking, about to sob.

"Okay, okay please... don't cry. We'll be more careful, I promise. So, I'll tell Chaz to expect us. And we'll make plans right away. We'll get info from Chaz and look into that school he's talking about. He also said he's sure his brother can get me into a restaurant out there. With the money from my tuition I'm sure we can cover the bills." Gina sniffles.

"This is exciting, right? I've got to sell my bike, pack my stuff and get to the bank. You'll need to tell your parents and do some stuff too, huh?"

"Are you kidding me? I'm not going." she says sternly.

"Ahh, c'mon Gina, it'll work out."

I reach to embrace her but she jerks away. I'm shunned, a first.

"Easy Gina, c'mon. You've got to come, we're a team." I say.

She lifts her chin up, and says with certainty, "Forget it Nick, I'm not going. All these years together I never knew you to be selfish. In fact, I know you never were."

I feel my anger rising. *Selfish?* How could she not understand that this is the right thing for us? She's being selfish, not me. This could be a great opportunity for us both. I'm dead set on this. I know this is right, I know it.

"Look, if you're not coming... fine. But things have changed. I'm gonna go. I'm sorry Gina but I got dreams, and... and I'm stepping into them, I have to. It's done... I'm going."

"What's gotten into you? You're being rude like your friends lately." she says, squinting through tears.

"Hey, it's my life. I'm going, you coming or not?" She looks me in the face.

"I thought it was *our* life *our* dream. And No, I'm not. You know when I think about it, it's been a long time since our childhood when I saw that angel on your shoulder." She turns away suddenly sobbing, then bolts out of the car and into the house.

She can't be serious. *She thinks I still believe, like some kid.*

Between her and my sister with praying, and angels, I wish they'd get real.

Across the yard her dad looks at me confused, concerned. I shrug my shoulders in reply. Man, am I glad she's not pregnant.

Chapter Five

Going to California

"Standing on a hill in my mountain of dreams…

~ Led Zepplin

It really sucks that I won't even see her before I leave. She's only a few miles away, and by this time tomorrow she'll be three thousand. My dusty mirror reveals how well my face has healed over the last few weeks—but does nothing to mask my tired eyes.

I've been waking up the last few nights with a clear memory of Gina and I when we were ten years old holding hands by the pond. And there seems to be no shaking it. It plays in my mind like some mystery. It's disturbing, yet I can't see why.

We were laying on the fresh green grass by the pond. In the warmth of the sun we pointed and gave names to passing cloud formations while listening to my pocket radio. Then, the first few words of Don Mclean came on.

"A long, long, time ago…" and the thrill of his song starting jolted us both. Her excited eyes turned to mine from the clouds, her curly hair kissed by the sun framed her pretty face and happy smile. Her joy was contagious, and I caught it. I turned the music up. Within seconds we were both up singing the first lines in tune to each other openly.

When the tempo increased and the refrain of "American Pie" was clearly on our lips, we started singing passionately into imagined microphones, like we were Sonny and Cher. The song's lyrics we knew well, what they all meant, we didn't. Still don't. Like what's *"your mortal soul"* anyway? Maybe that's where the mystery lies, in the music. We broke higher ground through his song that day, sealing that afternoon with our longest kiss to date. Leaving without her, feels like it may erase any trace of that joy we once shared together.

It will be like saying good-bye to a whole era of our innocence.

It's still hard to believe that we're actually broken up.

Pauly handed me a new *Hustler* magazine *"to take my mind off her."* That it did, for a very short time. I packed it along with a *Playboy* and a *Penthouse*. It's unbelievable, Pauly just walks into the drugstore where we've known the lady behind that counter since we were buying baseball cards and now he just slaps them on the counter ever since he turned eighteen it seems. Hustler's very different. Not just centerfolds anymore; there're guys in the mags with them now. The images from its glossy pages still roll around my mind like a slideshow, each one fighting for my attention. Two weeks was the longest Gina and I have gone without speaking or seeing each other, and that was over four years ago when she was at Girl Scout camp.

I tried to reach her but her mom says she doesn't want to talk. She still must be upset, 'cos her mom was short and to the point with me. And that's not like her mom.

The butterflies in my stomach are for real as I take a breath to curb my anxiety. I remember the coolest part of flying is taking off. I have a 4:35 PM flight to LA. With the three-hour difference in Pacific Time, I'll arrive at 6:30 PM or so, still an hour left before the sunsets.

Heading down the steps with my baggage, I see Uncle Lou helping Trisha with another jigsaw puzzle. She's listening to *Let It Be* again. My eyes roll instinctively. Soon I'll be so far from this song.

"Uncle Lou... hey, how ya doin'?"

"How *you* doin? You ready to fly? Be sure to chew gum or your ears will pop."

"Yeah, all set. I have gum." I check my watch then call up the stairs. "Hey Ma, come on, I don't want to miss the flight."

"Don't rush your mom. There's time before the flight," he says.

"Yeah I guess so." I relax a bit.

"Hey Nephew, be careful out there. I mean it." Uncle Lou's bushy eyebrows narrow to a sincere, or serious expression. I'm not quite sure which. "You know what they say about guys with earrings." He lifts his right arm and gently shakes a limp wrist.

Not you too, I think to myself. He looks 'Guido' with three buttons open, a heavy Christ head necklace resting on a thick mat of hair in the center of his chest.

"And I heard you can catch herpes, and people get pregnant in those spas you talk about ya know." His deep voice and Bronx accent can't hide the silliness of his statements at times. I just smile and shake my head. I love him, he's great.

"Trust me Unc, I'm not gonna get pregnant."

"You know what I mean, wise guy." Hard to believe he went to the same school with my Dad. He's been around for my mom a lot since my dad died.

Trisha suddenly gets up and shuffles over to me, both hands out, holding a small statuette, a Virgin Mary figurine.

"Here Nicky, keep Her with you... She's Queen of the Angels.... keep her with you. Remember us...okay. Okay, remember us, okay. And keep her with you. I'll... I'll miss you."

I pull a handkerchief from my dads old jacket that I'm wearing and wrap the Madonna in it, then put it back into the pocket. I go to hold her, but her condition almost always tends to make her pull away— it's like a sensory overload at times that makes it hard to show her affection. I don't understand it, but I kiss her on her head anyway.

"Yeah okay, sure. Thanks, Trish. I love you too... and I'm going to miss you."

She sinks her head, then raises it and speaks right to my face; her eyes wander a bit above and around me.

"If you love us, write to us. In words, okay, in words... okay, words."

"Okay, yeah sure Trisha," I say, anxious to go. She can't even read I think to myself.

I look at her, and I miss my Dad. Mom's carefully wiping tears from her cheeks with a kerchief as she heads down the stairs. The last time I saw her cry was at my Dad's funeral and the thought of that sucks. Her curly hairstyle bounces with each step down. Between her Sunday dress, lipstick, and jewelry, you'd think she's going out to dinner.

Uncle Lou greets her at the bottom and put's his arm around her, pulling her in.

"Oh Sis, don't cry, he'll be fine. He's a big boy, wearing a pretty earring," Uncle Lou says. He's not helping. She quickly turns to him while walking and puts her finger up to his face. They communicate with their hands as well as their mouths.

"Now Louie, don't forget to pick up Joey from practice, and order a pizza pie and salad for dinner and give Trish her medication."

"I got it covered Angel," he says. "And Nick be good, I mean it, and write to your sister and mother."

He wraps his arm around my shoulder and squeezes me in, then softly smacks my face with his other hand.

"You better behave out there, or I'll come out and kick your… you know what!"

"I'll behave, don't worry. Take care of them, okay? And I'll bring back the gold…promise."

My mom looks at me and suddenly seems very troubled.

"Nick what are you wearing? Where did you get that tee-shirt?"

I'm wearing a red and blue printed AC/DC on a white tank top under an open denim shirt.

"What's wrong? I made it in silk-screening class last year." I say.

"Well you're not wearing that to the airport," she says firmly.

"Come off it, Ma be serious. It's just a music group!"

"It's a tee-shirt and you better go change into a nice shirt, we're going out for lunch. Or you *will* miss the flight."

"Oh man, c'mon, really?" I dash up the stairs and I'm back down in no time with a polo shirt.

At the bottom of the stairs, my Mom gently takes my hand. And between her teary eyes and favorite perfume, I get choked up about leaving.

"Did you say good-bye to your sister?" she asks.

"Yeah…yes, I did."

"She was very upset this morning. She had a terrible dream. A nightmare."

"She seemed fine when we said 'so long' earlier. She gave me her statue."

"Well it was so disturbing; she woke me up and said 'someone is feeding the wicked wolf inside their house.' I'm troubled by it."

"Geez Ma…don't worry. It's probably the fairytales she's been hearing. Riding hood, or the three pigs, or something."

My mother slowly shakes her head. "I don't understand it."

"Ya know, Ma, I still get that nightmare from Fantasia once in a while. Remember when we went to see that with Pop?"

"Yes, of course. You were petrified of…of… I forget what character was it again, oh yes, 'Chernabog' the black god. Oh, you used to run to our bed quite a bit from that one.

"I thought it was the Devil. I don't know I was only five or six."

"It's Slavic folklore. Boy, he was scary for a cartoon."

"She'll be fine Mom, It's just a dream." Mom's tears have calmed and have been wiped dry.

"Well, you be careful out there. Be sure to call us as soon as you land in California. Let's go have a nice lunch before your flight."

I won't see Joey before I leave he's at wrestling practice. Said our good-byes before he left this morning. He's a good kid, a good wrestler. He'll do better than me in school, I can tell. He still has straight friends. Sometimes when I look at him I remember the day Dad died.

I hear his scream and clearly see the terror in his face. We all have our nightmares. That's one he and I share for sure.

****

It's not long before I'm sitting at a window seat near the wing of a Boeing 747 viewing the sky and the land in between the clouds. I pull out the Walkman that I got from Gina for Christmas last year. I recorded a bunch of great tunes onto a couple cassettes and labeled them "Nick's Mix."

Goin' to California starts up exactly the way I imagined it as I head West on a plane. An attractive blonde stewardess pushes a beverage cart stopping at every seat down the aisle. In a short time, she stops by me.

I gaze up and I'm immediately met by Barbie blue eyes and a cute doll face, with a small beauty mark high on her cheek. She reminds me of Ginger on *Gilligan's Island*. Her glossy lips move, but I can't hear what she's saying. I push pause and remove my headphones… "Excuse me?"

"Would you like a cold soft drink or cocktail?" Her voice is soft, seductive.

"Oh… sure, yeah. I'll have a Michelob."

"We carry only Budweiser, Miller and Becks," she says.

"Bud's fine… thanks."

She pulls a can out of ice from the beverage cart, lifts off the pop-top and throws it in the trash bag. I lower the tray in front of me as she tops the beer can with a plastic cup then places a napkin and a bag of nuts on the tray.

"That'll be three dollars please, sir."

No one's ever called me 'sir' before. It's weird.

"Sir? It's Nick, ma'am…." I hand her the money.

"Okay Nick, it's Debbie, not ma'am." She smiles.

"Debbie. Okay, got it." She's totally hot I think to myself.

She smiles again with sparkling eyes and as she turns her skirt flips, dancing off her butt from the spring in her step.

I can't help it and start undressing her with my eyes. I find myself doing that a lot lately. She glances over her shoulder and catches me checking her out. My eyes move up to her face as she's smoothing her upper lip with her tongue. She then winks right at me.

I have no idea on how to approach that; I mean I think she may even be old enough to be my mom. She's the blonde beach type you don't see in New York, and I've only seen on TV. Well, and in my Penthouse collection. I put my earphones back on, I'm really missing Gina.

I zone-out as Zeppelin strums their dreamy ballad in my ears. I close my eyes and my mind takes me to relive a camping trip with my father the summer before he died...

I'm taking in a beautiful sunrise over the Catskill Mountains. Tall evergreens surround a small, still lake where bullfrogs croak. A purple specked, blue neon dragonfly lands on the tip of my Dad's fishing pole that leans next to me. It's stunning colors, transparent wings, and precision landing amaze me as it sits, inches away.

I feel I'm one with it all, this rich grand environment, kind of heaven on earth. I'm peaceful. A mist hovers over the water as geese pass honking high overhead. The small campfire is burning low, I stir it, add wood and watch the sparks rise.

A loud splash snaps me out of my tranquil zone and I see the ring of ripples from the fish that just jumped. I rush into my Dad's pup tent and shake him. He barely stirs. I attempt to pull him out into the open air still in his sleeping bag.

"Hey Pop, c'mon get up! Let's go, the fish are jumping!

He slowly shuffles in his bag, turning.

"Whaa, no, no, okay, okay... sshh, sshh, sshh, you'll scare the fish," he says.

He rolls over and pulls the bag over his head.

"Oh no you don't, c'mon..." I insist.

I pull the zipper down the bag and as he feels the chill he suddenly pops up, rubbing his face and hands warming them. To my surprise, he lifts me up over his shoulder in a fireman's carry.

"You're right buddy, let's do this. Ya know, jump into it head first. Ready? Heeere weee go!" He beelines for the lake, freaking me out.

"No Pop don't...no please, put me dowwwnn," I cry.

He's about to toss me in the lake but grips me good and swings me around in a circle. I'm amazed at his strength. I'm thirteen and he just picks me up like he did years ago when I was little. He's always joking, having fun. Taking us places, playing games, telling jokes. I'm going to grow up to be just like him. My hero.

Later in the day, with poles over shoulders and fish on a stringer we head up to the campsite. My Dad turns to me, his strong arm around my shoulder then stops.

"You know, someone once said… *If you give a man a fish he eats for a day, but if you teach him to fish, he'll eat for a lifetime.*" he says.

And then hands me his favorite fishing pole.

"But remember you sometimes need to give the man a pole. Here you go."

"Really Pop, for me?"

"Yup it's yours now."

It's his favorite. He's caught many prize fish with it. It's a much better rod, with a very expensive reel on it. But the fact that he sees me responsible enough means so much. Even more than that, it's his— a personal gift to me.

He lifts up the stringer of trout. "Let's eat!"

We always keep our catch, if it's legal size. We freeze perch and sunfish for crabbing and fishing out on Long Island.

"Two hundred years ago the Indians didn't drag a fish through the water just to throw them back—they didn't play with their food," he says with a smile, then adding, "The very best restaurants can never serve fish fresher than this!"

I rinse off a couple of the trout I gutted and hand them to him. Then continue to gut the rest and put them on ice in the cooler.

My Dad stuffs plenty of fresh herbs from mom's garden into the trout's cavity, rosemary, garlic, lemon, thyme, and then some Kalamata olives. He sprinkles sea salt and olive oil on the skin and wraps the whole thing in foil. He places it on the grate next to the corn steaming right in their husks.

He adds a couple of plum tomatoes cut in half, thick wheels of red onions, sliced zucchini from the garden then brushes it all with olive oil. The fresh ciabatta bread he wrapped in foil would be warm and crusty from the coals when done. Fire to me is friendly, comforting, and always means we're going to eat soon. And in the evening, out here, its light and warmth– but my father fights it for a living in the city.

We sit rotating items on the grill, timing them so they come off together fresh and hot. I see him, like my Mom, use all his senses to know when the food is ready to serve *or even worthy to prepare.*

My parents always look, smell, taste and feel everything they buy to prepare. I see them do this in the market and always before throwing anything out. Which rarely happened. They were on the tail end of the Great Depression. Wasting food to them is not only disrespectful, but a sin. I'm impressed with his ease in cooking outdoors.

"Hey, Pop did you really learn how to cook at the firehouse?"

"Yup, and Grandma of course. But some of the best cooks I know are firemen."

I stoke the fire gently, igniting my stick. And suddenly am inspired.

"You know, I like to cook. Maybe I'll be a chef!"

"A chef, huh? Well, I see you helping your Mom a lot. You're a good cook."

"Why'd you want to become a fireman anyway?" I ask.

"A long story, but let's just say, I saw something that shouldn't have been."

"Like what?"

"Let's just say, I've seen some awful results from people who start fires. Many aren't by accident. It looks like it's the fires we're fighting, but many times it's the people behind them. Like arsonists, insurance frauds and landlords who want their tenants out. Many times, innocent people die. Lord knows we could use help. We need good people to step up. Ya know, more heroes." His large hand gently squeezes my knee. "*The good life*, is not as much about you, as it is about others… you'll see."

"Yeah? Then I want to be a hero…like you. I wanna be somebody."

"Hey… you are somebody, buddy, remember that." He smiles confidently. "You're so special. You're one of a kind son. Just believe you can achieve great things and never give up. And be sure to choose your friends wisely."

My insides swell with a warm fuzzy feeling to the point that it springs a huge smile of joy onto my face. "Thanks, Pop."

He puts his warm arm around me and pulls me close.

"So now, you'd like to be a chef? And a hero… hmmm, yeah… ya think?

"Yeah, I'd like to be a chef someday." I say.

"Well if you can feed people, then you could be their hero, right? Don't you think?"

"I guess." I feel self-conscious saying 'I want to be a hero'. Not sure if that's something you can choose ahead of time.

I reach over to my backpack and pull out a *Sports Illustrated* magazine, this years 1976 swimsuit edition, hoping to change the subject. I hand it to my Dad.

"Hey Pop, did you see this month's sports edition? Pauly just gave it to me."

Pauly has been getting Sports Illustrated mailed to his house as part of his Dad's subscription ever since we were eight years old. But the swimsuit edition, this year, at thirteen, was quite different, personal.

My Dad's eyes widen surprised as he sees twin sisters frolicking in swimsuits in the surf on the front cover. He flips through the pages; it's filled with the two girls posing in bikinis. My Dad's my best friend and I think it's so cool that I can share this with him. I'm sure he's gonna like it. I mean, it's Sports Illustrated, what guy wouldn't? 'Twice as Nice in Baja' it says on the front cover. Twins! I eagerly look to his face for his reaction.

But I'm not sure about the look I'm getting, definitely not a grin. He flips through faster and faster and then stops, like he's stunned.

"What the… what happened to all the sports," he says, looking to me sincerely. My excitement fades as I notice concern on his face.

"Buddy… buddy, bikini is not a sport. I know this seems like a good thing, but…"

Guess I was wrong. He moves closer, putting his arm around me again and speaks softly with concern.

"...Look, the world is full of temptation. Remember... we're men, we respect and protect women. That's someone's daughter, sister, and may be someone's mom one day, buddy. They're gifted so much deeper than their skin. Gee...it's important you see that. It's really not a spectator sport. Yeah, they're beautiful, but these photos..."

My Dad hesitates a moment and I see he's troubled. I don't know why.

"Geez it seems like just a few weeks ago you were only interested in playing with frogs and fireflies." He sighs.

"There's plenty of female athletes that really deserve the respect of that sports cover, and not just because they could wear a bikini. But I'm glad you brought it up because I believe we need to talk." He pulls me even closer.

"When I was in Catholic school, in the Bronx, a nun read a bible verse for us to discuss in class. From the book of Deuteronomy, she read. '*This day* I have set before you, life and death, the blessing and the curse, so choose life, so you and yours will live.'

"It was Sister Cecilia. She was Native American, petite, lighthearted, very kind and well respected. She quoted a Cherokee saying from her childhood to help explain the verse to us clueless ten-year-olds." I listen closely.

"She said, 'We all have two hungry wolves fighting fiercely for control inside of us. One feeds on anger, greed, deceit, evil, and leads to poverty, to death. The other feeds on joy, peace, generosity, truth, virtue, and leads to prosperity, to life.' Then she said something I'll never forget."

'The battle will get violent, but you choose who wins, because it'll be the wolf that *you* feed. And will then forever live with.'

"We really need to be careful what we feed our minds Nick, because eventually it can fill your heart. *No man can serve two masters.* We will either act out in love, or in lust."

88

He gently tosses the magazine into the fire and it flares up to my horror.

"No Dad wait... Oh man, I... I so do love them!"

"You don't even know them."

"And that was Pauly's!"

"Well you tell Pauly to talk to me. I'll pay him for it."

"Now... let me tell you about your mom. How our strong friendship, faith, and patience led to true love first, a healthy marriage... and how that love, led to having you."

He rips the hot crusty bread in half and passes one to me...

I slowly open my eyes.

The emptiness of my beer can echoes as I place it down onto the snack tray in front of me. It lands much louder than expected and when I look up away from my thoughts, I have Debbie's attention from several rows up, she smiles. My eyes immediately gravitate to her cleavage and I gaze a few moments before moving down to her long legs below her skirt. My thoughts are way past Sports Illustrated. I snap myself out of it and glance back up to her face and smile.

I rise up from my seat and head to the rear bathrooms.

Looking in the mirror, I light a cigarette, and then turn to pee. Within seconds a screeching alarm goes off right above my head.

A moment later a stewardess swings open the door. While I'm peeing, I freeze with the cigarette in my mouth, penis in hand, in full view of the stewardess.

"Put that cigarette out now," she says, before slamming the door.

I'm shaking. I don't get it. Every plane to Florida was full of smokers, and had no smoke alarms. I zip up my jeans, rinse my hands and straighten myself up, hoping to slip out and back into my seat unnoticed. But Debbie, another stewardess, and all the people in the back turn and stare at me as I return to my row.

I sheepishly slide into my seat. Debbie soon nears.

"So young man, remember, no smoking on this flight."

"Yeah, I got it. Why the hell are there ashtrays everywhere then?"

"This flight is no smoking. Would you like another beer?"

"No thanks. I may just recline a bit." I say.

"Okay. Let's make you comfy."

She opens the storage bin above my head and starts to stretch for something. The hem of her skirt slowly rises, inches away from my face revealing her upper thighs as she leans onto the tips of her toes. For some reason, I think she's doing this on purpose. I read about this stuff in Penthouse Forum. I have to stop my hand from reaching out to caress her inner thigh. I turn my head, but now my gaze is on her breasts, which are above my head as she's stretching to reach the bin above. I feel awkward cause this is hard for me to handle. This woman who's old enough to be my mom is seriously turning me on— and practically an inch from being on top of me.

She pulls out a small pillow and a blanket, shuts the bin, and then settles back onto her heels. She leans over me, her ample cleavage right above my chin, her scent is sweet, perfumed.

She tucks the pillow behind my head and gently squeezes both my shoulders. Then slowly slides her soft hands down my arms to my elbows.

"There you go. This will help you rest. Comfy?" She places the blanket on my knees.

"Oh yeah. Thanks." I can't resist focusing on her butt as her skirt flips up off it. I capture the image and close my eyes.

I awake to a voice on the intercom.

"Ladies and gentlemen, we'll be landing in Los Angeles shortly. Please remain seated, fasten your seatbelt and all seats should be in an upright position. It's a sunny, seventy-five degrees, and clear skies. Thank you for flying with TWA."

In several minutes, the plane touches down with a landing that is short and sweet. I see and hear the passengers clapping; I can only assume they're applauding the landing. I don't get it. Must be a Hollywood, West Coast thing?

Immediately people stand, lining up to exit the plane. I gather my stuff. As soon as the exit door opens people begin filing out. I somehow end up the last in line. I'm about to pass Debbie as she welcomes people to LA as they exit. She places her fingers lightly in the center of my chest causing me to stop. She smiles and places a folded piece of paper in my shirt pocket, leans into my ear and whispers.

"Welcome to L.A. Nick. If you need to know where the party is, just call." I nod, acknowledging the note.

Her warm breath, soft voice, and scent entice me and my blood's rushing. I turn my head to her as I pass and she winks at me again. Instinctively I try to wink back, but it fails, distorting my whole face. I never winked before. She stifles her laugh, bites her bottom lip as I feel my face blushing. I take my first step out of the plane into the welcoming warmth of L.A.

Chapter Six

Long Time

"I've got to keep on chasin' that dream,
though I may never find it…"

~ Boston

Standing still, with my hand on the rail, I descend diagonally into a sea of people. It's a lot brighter here than at JFK back in New York. It's not the lights but the brighter colors dotted throughout the luggage area, on shorts, skirts, caps, and shirts. Bright white smiles and golden hair are more than I ever saw in one place before.

I scan the area and immediately see Chaz with a huge grin on his chiseled face. He looks totally Californian with a purple tank top, yellow shorts, and a deep tan.

He shoots both arms into the air over the crowd and starts heading towards me. We high five, a loud clap echoing through the terminal, and laugh out loud, giving each other a friendly shove. He grabs my carryon bag.

"Any dirt weed in here?" he asks curiously.

"Yeah, I bought some weed from Patsy."

"Well good news, we're not smoking anymore of Patsy's dirt weed," he says, smiling.

"This way bro, c'mon." We head over to a circle of people, three deep around a baggage carousel and wait for my two bags.

"This is awesome dude," My eyes focused outside. "Last time I saw palm trees that size was when my Dad flew us to Florida."

"Well, welcome to the "left coast" dude. Plenty of those! I'm totally psyched for you man!"

A cigarette hangs on my lip as I rummage through my shirt pocket for a light. I find Debbie's number.

"Hey, check this out… a stewardess's number. Oh, yeah, and I was naked with another."

"That's it Dude. Dream on, Nick. You just keep dreaming."

95

"I kid you not. Here it is see… Debbie, she wants to party. The other one walked in when I was peeing, shocked the hell out of me. She stared at my pud."

"No way! Hahaha… she saw your pud bro?" Chaz has a near full belly laugh.

"I'm dead serious, dude." Felt real awkward, only Gina's seen me out of my pants.

"Wrong… I have too! Hey, call her up; see if she has a friend. C'mon, hook me up."

"Don't know man. I miss Gina. I was kinda rough on her. We're not even talking. I tried, but she didn't want to." I said some things I shouldn't have.

"I'm tossing it out Dude." As I go to crumble it up I smell her perfume.

"Give it to me bro, don't toss it out." I lift it to my nose and her scent is stronger. My mind takes me to a clear picture of her lip-gloss, blue eyes, and cleavage.

"Yeah. Maybe your right." I fold it neatly and place it back in my pocket. "You never know."

My baggage stands out on the carousel. One's a big old green army duffle bag that has my knives, cookbooks, some towels, jackets, shoes, and stuff. The other a large light blue suitcase that's been in the basement at our house forever, and is holding my clothes.

"So, you and Gina are not talking, huh? Never thought I'd hear that," Chaz asks.

"Yeah, me neither."

"Hey, why don't you surprise her with a plane ticket for Thanksgiving, or spring break? She'll be over it by then."

"Heyyy… yeah that's a plan. Spring break. Yeah, I'll cop a ticket for her." That's months away we'll be talking by then. Can't hurt to try.

"Did you sell your bike? I got my eye on some wheels for you."

"Yeah, Philly bought it. Who knows where he got the cash, I was afraid to ask."

We walk up to the back of a silver Plymouth Horizon and he unlocks the hatchback, popping it open. We throw my bags in and slam it shut. I'm here. It's done.

"How do you like my wheels? I got AC."

"Very nice…like it, sporty."

I hop into a bucket seat, roll down the passenger window and stick my elbow out. There's beer cans in the back, an ashtray filled with butts, and half joints. I feel at home already.

His tires screech and squeal against the cement pavement as we descend around each bend to the ground level.

"It's so good to see you man and I'm really psyched to be here!" I slap him in the back of the head.

"Ouch… geez man. My bro says he could hook you up with a hot restaurant that's opening soon, if you're interested."

"Really, he said that?" I met Chaz's brother a couple of times when he visited New York. He's like five years older than us. Dates a lot of different chicks.

"He said big names are gonna go there. Some spa-type California food just like you've been saying. Don't screw it up 'cos he'll kill me. I told him you're serious and he knows you've been cooking in New York for a few years already.

"Are you kidding me dude?" I feel an anxious rush of excitement.

"Not at all. I knew you'd need work, so I asked him." He shrugs his shoulders. "No big deal."

"Whoa… don't worry, I'll work my ass off. They could pay me nothing and I'd be happy."

"Well the chances are you'll be paid close to that to start." I'm so happy to see him, it's great to see his bright white grin again.

"Thanks man, thank you. That's unreal, too cool. And thank your brother for me."

"You thank him. I figured we'd party for a week until you get settled and then give him a call." He handes me a big joint.

"Now that's a fatty." It's as thick as my pinky.

"Light up, more where that came from. This dude I know grows it in his closet."

I eject *Nick's Mix* from my Walkman and pop it into the car cassette player. *Long Time* by Boston is just beginning on the tape. I light up, take a huge hit, and then hand it to Chaz.

He hits it as he exits onto an upward ramp for an interstate 405, a freeway; as the song progresses, so does his speed.

He reaches the top of the ramp and I see us merging into the biggest highway I've ever seen, packed with thousands of cruising cars. We're suddenly in the current of this multiple-lane river of red taillights flowing north.

"We're lucky… there's no traffic tonight."

"No traffic?" I laugh as cars are packed in both directions.

"Nope. We're moving dude! The traffic out here usually sucks, bro."

"Great tune, crank it up!"

I knew he'd like my mix. I reach to turn it up and see a highway sign for Hollywood. Chaz slaps my knee as he's exhaling smoke. I stick my fist out the window and pump it into the air towards the sign and marvel at a perfect row of tall palm trees highlighted by the sun.

Yeah, I believe this side is greener. I'm certain now it holds the answer to my dreams, my future; it must, because I'm feeling right about it…

I inhale the joint and slowly exhale it through my nostrils, savoring the aroma of one of my favorite herbs. The most popular one in the restaurant business I've learned.

****

Fagots Stay Out... reads the misspelled wooden sign above a beer tap, across from the stool where I'm seated. Don't know how I missed it before. Looks like it's been there forever. Along with old dusty license plates, signage, and photos that have accumulated all over this sticky place for years...part of its story I guess. It's obviously not an issue, or enforced by management.

I pull an ashtray closer and light a smoke. This is the very first-place Chaz took me to in Los Angeles, perfect for beer and shots. Over the months I've met rebels, rockers, and writers along with chefs, bartenders, and wait staff from around town. The crowds kept fresh, by mixing with the latest starry eyed arrivals who move into LA daily — all types, from all over the world. It's a fact many famous people ate and drank here over the years. Jim Morrison being the most notorious, getting kicked out for pissing on the bar.

I fit right in. There are plenty of guys with earrings and they're not all gay. Some dudes have them in both ears...*what's that all about?*

Since *Prego* opened months ago they've been weeding out some of the original cooks. I'm advancing as the positions need to be filled. The main chefs couldn't care less about a college degree. They like hard workers, who are willing to learn, and who love the craft. Plenty of eager Latinos.

It seems they prefer people just willing and able, to ones who think they're chefs because of a couple years in school. Many of those guys are lost without their recipes and thermometers.

I once read, 'Reading recipes to a chef, is like painting by numbers to an artist.' My mom's an artist. She could write the book. It takes courage, imagination, and creativity to write the book. She's got that. Most people just look to understand them. I'll take imagination over intellect any day.

The restaurant is extremely busy, gaining a high-end Beverly Hills clientele. I'm doing a lot of hours that I don't mind a bit. Cooks are knocking at the door daily to get into this kitchen.

And they would work for nothing, which is a little less than what I'm making. It's tough but if I stick this out I know it will open many kitchen doors for me.

I'm off tomorrow and going swimming over at Debbie's. She has this cool backyard that surrounds a kidney-shaped pool lined with stone and tropical plants like it's out of a Tarzan movie or something. It's been months and I haven't heard a word from Gina. I've left messages, written postcards, and tried to hold out for a while, but a man has his needs. I broke down and called Debbie. She has been eagerly fulfilling them. She's such a knockout – pretty, cool, and loves to party. I'm past the fact that she's as old as my mom; it's strictly casual sex.

She's turning me onto some new things I've seen in the mags but wouldn't dare try with Gina. But it sure has given me an appetite for more.

Debbie's been working long hours and told me she does a little cocaine once in a while to get through the long days. I've been hearing a lot about it lately.

I know some of the cooks are doing it at work. The rich and famous seem to be all over it as well. It's the rich man's drug, they say.

I'm working very long hours this season and was just asked to work my day off. One of the head chefs asked me to assist him with some magazine photo shoots. Food design. Just the fact that he asked me is an honor. I mean, it's like he's taken me under his wing with this.

"Last call!" echoes across the bar. I look at my empty shot glass and signal the bartender for a double. I wish they'd close at four like back East. Two o'clock is too soon after work.

****

In less than ten hours I'm lounging on Debbie's pool patio. Half a doobie in the ashtray on the cocktail table next to me, and a cold beer in hand. A long cord wanders from the house through the patio doors connecting the phone that's on the table too. It's cool, new push button numbers. Touch tone they call it. I could dial New York fast, ten digits in only ten seconds. *I got to get my mom one of these.*

Debbie has no problem with me calling long distance. But the high cost has been my excuse to my mom for not calling her more often. The phone rings.

"Hello..." It's her.

"Ma! Hey Ma… how you doing?"

"Nickeee! Oh, honey, I'm so glad you called."

I miss hearing her. And that goes for hearing any New York accent. Voices I feel I can trust; At least I know where they're coming from. Who the hell knows where anybody who lives here is from?

"How's things at home? Where's Trisha and Joey?"

"Oh Nicholas, you missed them again. They're in school. But we're fine, all fine, Honey. We miss you!"

"Miss you too Ma. Did Joey get the birthday card I sent?" I place my beer down to ratchet up the back of my lounge chair.

"Yes, yes, he was thrilled, very generous of you. He wanted to treat Trisha to somewhere fun, like to a movie or bowling with it. But I insisted he save it, or buy himself a new helmet or something."

"Did you get the postcards I sent from Hollywood?"

"I did, thank you. Looks like so much to see and do out there."

101

"Sooo much to see. It's warm and sunny, like every day. I'm not kidding It hasn't even rained yet."

"No rain in months? Gee I can't imagine. So are you ready to come home?

"No Ma, I can't. This restaurant is so busy. I'm working, learning so much; I'm really liking it. And guess what? Good news."

"What is it Honey?"

"I was asked to assist the head chef with his photo shoots. He designs dishes for various magazines. I'm working with him and getting paid extra. Start next week."

"Oh honey, that's wonderful! They must really like you. Ohhh, I'm so happy for you." I'm happy too, that at least she knows I'm moving up.

"You should just keep going and write a cookbook. Why not? Your father would be so proud. Don't forget what your high school teacher told you, you should keep on writing."

"Yeah, yeah, I'm nowhere near writing a cookbook. But I'll never forget what else that teacher said. That I was the biggest waste of talent she ever met."

"Well, Nicholas, you kept playing hooky from her class."

"Yeah, let's face it, Ma, what's writing gonna do for me anyway? You can't eat paper. I'm learning a lot from the chefs. You're the one who should write the cookbook. You're the best. I'm your biggest fan. Maybe I can help you get the recipes down." I prime my lips with a sip of beer.

"But really, when are you coming home to visit, honey? We miss you. We look forward to Christmas so we can see you." Oh no... She's not going to like this.

"Oh yeah well, ehem. Yeah Mom. I'm really sorry— I can't come home for Christmas. I was told I have to work. They say there are so many holiday parties booked that there's no way anyone can take off during that season. Everyone is expected to work."

The silence on her end is painful for me. I know she feels crushed and imagine her bottom lip jutting out with disappointment. We're always together for every holiday. And I already missed this year's Thanksgiving. I try to change the subject.

"Hey mom have you seen Gina around? She hasn't returned my calls and I thought she had my new number." I'm hoping to get any info on Gina I can. I really miss talking to her.

"I haven't seen her Nick. She used to visit us almost every day after you left. But I haven't seen her since she started school. I don't know what happened with you two, but she seemed very upset when you left. She's such a good kid. Trisha really misses seeing her and singing songs together." She sighs. "And no one should have to work Christmas, if I was out there I'd have a word with your boss!"

"C'mon Ma. Someone has to do it. And they pay extra for the holidays. We may even get bonuses. And Gina's probably too busy with school to visit you guys right now."

Debbie steps through the sliding glass door. Her long tanned legs in tight, white hot pants. She looks like a Dallas cheerleader. Her baby blue loose satin top matches her bright blue eyes and blonde hair. She sits next to me holding a mirror with thin white lines of cocaine, and puts it down next to my beer.

"Look, Ma I gotta go, please give a hug to Trisha and Joey for me." I'm very uneasy, nervous seeing the cocaine.

"Well…ehem, who knows? Maybe I can afford to fly all of you out here for Christmas in January. I hear Santa Claus wears shorts here."

"Oh that's silly, Santa in shorts." My eyes are stuck on Debbie. "I'm so sorry you missed the kids. You're all they talk about. Just be careful, NO drinking and driving, I mean it Nicholas. Please be good, we love you… and call!"

"I know, yeah, okay, love you too, Ma. Bye." I quickly override the guilt feeling I have of speaking to my Mom, as I'm about to break the law.

After hanging up, I take a big swig of beer. Debbie leans into the mirror and inhales a line through a rolled-up dollar bill. Her breasts, braless, I can clearly see through the low neckline of her blouse. She soon rises, grinning, pinching her nostrils.

"Here you go…" she sits upright and hands me the bill. "Just inhale like half the line at a time, it'll sting a little."

I'm nervous, feels wrong. I override my conscious.

"You know a lot of chefs are doing this now," I say. It's around a lot— can't be that bad.

"I don't know many people who aren't doing it, really," she says as she sinks into the lounge chair in her hot pants and blue top. It takes my mind back to a clear picture of a skin flick I saw, *Debbie Does Dallas*.

"Okay, let's see what all the hype is." I follow her lead and lean into the cocaine, inhaling a small amount. It stings my nose like she said it would, and then enters my nasal passage producing an interesting rush to my mind. I look at her smiling at me.

"Yeah…yes, yes." All's well. I lean in and inhale the rest, acting like I'm a rock star.

Chapter Seven

God Only Knows

"So what good would living do me…"

~ The Beach Boys

Gina

December, New York.

THE BEACH BOYS ECHO FROM the radio in my room as I brush my hair in the bathroom mirror. It's one of the most beautiful songs, and I haven't heard it in a while. I remember playing it over and over when I was in junior high school. So much in fact it started to skip, funny how Nick's near them in California now. Listening to it almost makes me cry, I miss him.

I close my eyes tight to hold back the tears, *happy thoughts, please, please, please... only happy thoughts.* In a moment, I'm transported, snuggling up to Nick on a quiet, sandy beach, all comfy on a soft beach blanket. The salty air in the warm ocean breeze is very relaxing as we're in awe of a spectacular sunset. I quickly sit at my desk, pull out my stationary and cling to those thoughts as I write, to Nick...again.

Dear Nick,

I'm listening to the Beach Boys and thinking of you out there in California. Curious if it is all that they say it is. Maybe I'll find out someday.

I'm starting to get used to my new 'bob' hairstyle and color. It's short but I like it a lot. So much so that I'm starting to think that blondes really do have more fun. It certainly gets a lot of attention. Not that I'm trying to, but it is kinda nice. Mom says it was impulsive to cut my hair after you left. Dad said he liked it better long, you know how old fashioned he is. But I didn't need to think twice about it. I wanted it and I needed change.

Watching most of my hair drop to the floor that day brought me to tears. But change is good; the style fits and people like me blonde. So, I just may fit right in out there! School's not quite working out like I wished, I think I may need to take a year off and go back next year, we'll see. I'd like to talk to you. I need to talk you.

I suddenly choke up with emotion. *Don't cry…don't cry…don't cry.* I drop the pen and jump up. I can't do this now. I need to get ready, finish my make-up. It's getting late.

Holding my mascara, I lean in to my mirror, careful not to get it all over my eyelid. Hmm…why did I even start wearing makeup anyway? It's a pain in my butt! It's like I have to, because everyone else does. Then, I have to take it all off. Boy, men just don't understand what we go through. Hhmm, I need some jewelry, maybe a couple of bracelets, and I'm good to go.

I open my desk drawer lift the top of my jewelry box and see a Quaalude. I forgot Patsy gave me this one a while ago. My first was a few months ago at a club. My anxiety was so overwhelming because of the crowds squeezing past, touching and pushing. It was a bad panic attack. I remember the music was so loud it vibrated the floor and it was impossible to hear or speak to my friends. I was practically in tears before I retreated to a corner to get away from it all. That's when Patsy and the girls convinced me to take a half of one just to relax. They all took them and seemed fine. They've been taking them for months already.

It did, it helped me relax. Being in the middle of that crazy scene was now tolerable. All the girls take them before going out now. I did

it with them a few times after that but not in a while— I wasn't planning on it tonight but, what the heck. It slips from my fingers as I go to
place it on my tongue, it drops down then bounces hard off my desk.

My eyes try to follow it, bringing me to my knees to find it. Okay…
there it is… up against my trash basket in front of my desk. I stretch
hard to get it, but it's just out of reach. My leg suddenly cramps up,
hurting so bad that I quickly go to straighten it and… Whack! My
head hits the desk so hard it stuns me. I try to smooth it as the throbbing increases, while my cramp painfully stiffens my leg even more.

In a moment, I become clearly aware of what I'm doing. *I'm on my
knees reaching for an illegal drug that I want.* It hits me like a kick in
my stomach, I feel sick. Just relax, and breathe for a moment.

God, what am I doing? I breathe deeply again, gently calming the
upset in my belly.

I go around my desk to pick up the pill. Part of me really wants
it, but I realize it sure as hell isn't the better part of me. I run to the
toilet and quickly flush it, no second thoughts. I was fine without
them, never needed them before. I just want to go out to see this
band tonight.

Thank heaven for my conscience, second time today. I sit at my
desk and pick up my pen to finish Nick's letter. Before I could write
another word, a car horn beeps loudly outside. I quickly fold up the
letter and put it with the other letters to Nick that I never mail, filling
my deep desk drawer.

"GINA!" My mother.

"Yeah Mom!" I slide the drawer shut.

"Your friend… that guy is outside, and if he beeps one more time
I'm gonna smack that kid… I don't know what you see in him."

"Okay. Okay, I'm coming. Be right down." I say, slipping into my
new heels.

"And Nick called again. I'm leaving his new number on the kitchen table. Your father and I are leaving now; we're going to the movies. Don't be out late again."

"Okay mom, you two have fun."

"Have a good night. Remember, 2AM!"

I tug my new skirt down, put on some lip-gloss and head towards the stairs.

"Okay. Thanks, Ma!" I yell from the top bannister, glad I won't have to slip past her in my outfit. She doesn't approve of what I've been wearing to clubs lately. I usually leave covered up in a coat.

As the front door clicks shut I safely walk down to the kitchen in my miniskirt. She really doesn't think I could be serious with Patsy. *Does she?* He's just a friend I've known, like, forever. I've been a bit confused without Nick, being single. They say the clubs in Manhattan are where things are really happening, but they make me uncomfortable, I see another side of people, I'm not sure I like. It's like they change at night.

My whole life to this point has been built with Nick. But these last few months well… he's changed about things that I know he truly cares about, feelings about family for one.

I open the note Mom left for me on the kitchen table.

Honey,

What has been your problem lately? And why are you with that boy? Nick IS trying to reach you. The ball is in your court. He said to call him when you can – His numbers on the back. Don't be out all night! 2 a.m. the latest!

Love You,
Mom

A long steady car horn is now blasting outside. Boy, he's lucky my mom's gone.

Looking over the note again, I'm comforted. This time I'm keeping it; it's time to call. I'll have to tell Nick about my visit to the clinic— Hmm... *California.* I fold the note with Nick's number and slip it into my purse.

Patsy's sitting in his dented orange Gremlin.

Geez, what a name for a car. As I get closer to the driver's side he sticks his head out the window. Oh boy… he has an earring.

"Look at you with the pierced ear." It's very unbecoming.

"Yeah, ever since I saw Nick's, I thought a lot about it."

"Where'd you get it?" it's a big black cross dangling on a chain.

"That head shop in the mall, next to the arcade." He flips his shaggy hair over his shoulder.

"You know that's the *right* ear?"

"Yeah so…?"

I just drop it. He doesn't know and I don't care at this point. He was no doubt wasted when he got it; he's usually stoned. He just looks over at me confused. Sometimes I feel sorry for Patsy.

We grew up together. I knew him way back when. Before all the drugs and stuff. He was always a kind, good kid. It's sad to see him screw up and drop out of high school thinking there's a future in this. I pray he grows out of it.

He pulls out a wad of cash and flips through it.

"Check this out. Look at all the money I made this week selling weed." I don't like the fact that he can get arrested. But I'm more concerned that he probably consumes more drugs than he sells and whatever he sells isn't helping people. I hate the fact that Nick smokes pot now. He extends his hand out the driver's side window to me as I approach the car.

"Hey, I copped a new batch of Lemmon 714's. Really good 'ludes!

111

You want a couple?" I think how a few months ago he never would have dared to ask me that. But after that night I took half of one at the club he hasn't stopped. The fact that I'm tempted to take it is bothersome.

It *would* help deal with the crowds, though. Quickly I scrub such a lie from my mind.

I feel torn, at odds like in my room. Maybe I shouldn't go out to-night. I could make that call to Nick; it's still early out there. But I've been waiting to see this band for a month.

"You sure you don't want?" Patsy asks, pill in hand.

"Yeah… No . No. Thanks. I'm okay Patsy. Just wanna meet the girls and see the band." It's one night only. *Adam and the Ants,* and I can't wait to see the outfits the girls are wearing.

He pops the pill in his mouth. And lifts up a bottle of beer to me.

"Well here then, at least have a beer. I got a bottle of JD under the seat if you want."

"No… Jack Daniels, geez. You know I don't drink hard liquor. Really, I'm fine. No one could ever say Patsy's not generous with his drugs and alcohol.

He insists, opening his hand with another pill.

"Come on, party a little with me. I'm telling you these biscuits are tops."

I'm enticed again but I quickly scratch it. The pills are thick and round and I see why 'biscuit' is the nickname. Sometimes I think Patsy eats them for breakfast.

"No, honestly, I'm good right now," I say.

He shrugs his shoulders and swigs his beer.

"Whatever… we could stop by my bro's place on the way down to the Ritz and get some coke, I'll buy if you wanna try."

"No. I don't want to 'try'. I wish you'd stay clear from all that stuff

Pat, you could get into a lot of trouble." *Cocaine? Geez, I would never.* "No stops, let's just get down there. It's gonna be packed."

I feel energized with every choice I make not to give into his peer pressure. I go around to the passenger side and slide into the seat. Can't wait to see this band tonight.

Patsy grinds the car into gear, then pops the clutch, which lunges it forward into the curb and us toward the dashboard.

"Whoahh! Gee whiz Patsy. Are you okay?"

"Yeah, yeah, I'm cool. Jus' need a new clutch."

He struggles straightening out the wheel as he grinds it into second, popping it again. I dig out the seatbelt that's buried in the crease of the seat.

"You better get that fixed."

Within minutes, we're passing by Nick's house.

"Saw Nick's mom at the gas station the other day," he says.

"Oh, ooh. How is she?" I ask.

"Don't know we didn't speak. She looks good though."

"You didn't ask? Not even about Nick, at all?"

"Didn't think about it. I was buying rolling papers."

Gee… I sure miss them all, especially Trisha, she's such a sweetheart. She amazes me at what she knows, her insights. Haven't visited since school began in the city. I'll stop for a visit tomorrow after mass.

Looking into my purse I take a quick peek at Nick's new number. It's only like six o'clock out there. I want to call him. Earlier today I looked at a photo of us at Confirmation. I had to tape it back together. I regretted, tearing it in half that first week we broke up.

The picture where we look like a little bride and groom in our Communion outfits I keep in my purse. I love that photo. I imagined us married that day.

That first innocent kiss grew so naturally into a true friendship. The day I promised myself to him I knew that *true* love is real, and if it's to be true, then I need to forgive. After that, I'm certain we can work it out.

I'm suddenly disturbed as to why I've been going out a lot with Patsy. I have no interest in him, no future ahead with him. It's strictly like a ride into the city. I know he's an old friend but not the person I need right now. I have to tell him that we shouldn't hang out anymore. I mean, I really need to sort things out and he sure isn't helping.

I'm still not sure how to process this chapter in my life, kind of a train wreck at times. But I believe in an instant all can be well. I still believe in miracles.

Looking at Patsy behind his earring and messy long hair I can see his young face, the one I remember. That kid in grade school who always used to make me laugh out loud. Now well…he's not as funny.

"You sure you don't want to stop by my brother Quinn's and get some blow?"

"Yeah Patsy, I'm sure, geez… enough with the drugs already." It seems his only focus lately. This year in college, we lost several students to heroin overdoses already, and two to suicide, very sad premature deaths that were preventable.

I recently prayed for Nick. It wasn't easy for him dealing with his Dad's death. I'm the one he always talked to about it. I wish we spoke before he left. Because I believe when I do reach out to him, there's a good chance we could pick up where we left off. I just hope he's not interested in anyone. He can't be. I mean, after all, he's been trying to contact me since he left.

Instinctively I touch my purse. I can almost feel the weight of the note. God only knows.

Chapter Eight

Highway to Hell

"Going down, party time…"

~ AC/DC

NICK

Los Angeles,

IT'S DECEMBER, THE TOP'S DOWN and it's a sunny seventy-two degrees out. I turn into the studio parking lot. The summer really doesn't end. My tan just deepens from when it started months ago. The constant rays are lightening my hair; it's slightly blonde on the sides now. Not a single drop of rain in months. Don't miss it one bit. I leave my roof off.

Walking into the studio for a photo shoot knowing the chef won't be here today is unnerving. He's dealing with an emergency issue that popped up at an important event at the art museum. Even though I know how to prepare the dishes he needs photographed, I mean I make them daily at the restaurant, he knows the ins and outs.

With the chef, I learn some new trick or technique that always helps to improve the photo. I do find confidence in knowing I have Polaroid pictures that he gave me showing step by step how to plate them if I need them.

The AC blows a refreshing breeze past my face and neck as I enter the kitchen with my tackle box full of knives, ready to work.

The surroundings familiar; I've been here several times before. A staged setting with lights, wires, sound equipment and cameras.

There's a large working studio kitchen in the center of this stage that's used for cooking shows, commercials, classes, as well as a variety of magazines who rent it for still photo shoots as well.

Lionel's leaning against a large stainless fridge smiling; he's a tall thin guy with a tight fro. His glasses magnify his happy eyes. His toothy smile and thick pink lips, contrast radiantly against his dark brown skin. He's flipping through my notebook. He's a professional photographer, freelance, for various magazines, close to seven years now. Working mainly with food stylists and some popular chefs. I'm energized working in this whole scene, being a fan of food mags since I can remember. He's ten years older and no stranger, in fact we quickly found common ground. He really likes weed too.

He's holding up my notebook. *How the hell did he got my notes?* I place my toolbox onto a stainless prep table and I toss my chef coat over it.

"Hey Lionel… what's up brother?"

"Hey, this is what's up. What is this… you been daydreaming?" He slaps his hand down loud on the table next to my stuff angrily.

Instinctively, my shoulders jolt. "What the… Where'd you get that anyway?"

"Don't ever stop dreaming my man. A lot of these notes are deep and that's a lucrative craft... work it. And if you ever get serious about it... I know a few people." He smacks the notebook again against his hand.

"And the concept for that resort spa place sounds cool, with the gourmet kitchen and in-house cinema and all. Don't lose this, my man, you may be onto something. Keep writing it down. Catch it. Imagination and inspiration can slip past if you're too busy bro.

He hands me the notebook. I fold it over, pop open my tool box, and throw it in.

"Yeah, that came to me when I was prepping the other day. I've been so busy lately I didn't even realize I forgot it… been adding notes to that plan for years now."

"Well, ideas come from somewhere. And if it helps people, then it's from somewhere good, and it's worth listening to."

Yeah, I guess. Well it's a start anyway. A dream I have with a girlfriend, back East."

I pull out the work sheet from the chef and open it up to review.

"The chef sent me solo today. There's an emergency at an event across town. He went over everything with me."

"Whoa, you're the chef today huh? Excuse me… 'Food Designer' He trusts you, my man. Cool, very cool. Future looking bright."

"Hey, it's his work, I'm just delivering the goods."

I've known Lionel a couple of months now and I respect him quite a bit. He's cool, encouraging, professional, talented, and he knows his craft. He encourages me all the time, and he loves to party. We usually smoke a bone right after the shoots as soon as the chef splits.

"You know, Lionel, I've been reading food magazines since I was a kid. I can't believe I'm preparing food for one now. I never even made it to college."

"I hear you man. College didn't get me this gig. Couldn't afford it. Sometimes I think the boys in charge want to try and keep us stupid. Just pay their bills while the best positions go to their family or friends, credentials or not. I've seen a lot of rich fools in charge of things."

Lionel unpacks his equipment, looking over each piece carefully as he pulls them out then extends his tripod legs to the floor. He's got a Nikon camera, with a variety of lenses that he loves. He uses the best color film, he says, *Kodachrome*. His magazine prints are bright, flawless.

"Okay, let's rock and roll. Show me what you got."

I pull out the items necessary for the first shoot from the cooler I brought in from work, a rack of lamb. Everything is trimmed and the finest cuts. Lionel will snap many shots stopping me at various steps along the way.

Forcing a stainless-steel rod carefully through the center of a rack of lamb I create a channel in the length of the loin. After tasting the simple stuffing mixture of shallot butter, chopped spinach and mint,

119

I mix in a little salt and white pepper then pack it neatly into the loin. Then generously sprinkle the whole outside with fresh ground rosemary mixed with salt and ground pink peppercorns. I then sear it in a hot sauté pan, top-side down. Within minutes, flip it and toss it into the oven to finish cooking.

Lionel stops me at times and clicks away with the camera at different points of the prep but the end product is what usually makes the pages.

"So, Bro, what are you serving with that today?" He asks.

"The lamb…uh, it's served with a butternut, sage, browned butter risotto. Oh, and braised baby herbed artichokes."

It's the last of the Autumn season menu. The menu changes seasonally even if the climate doesn't.

Next I pull out a wrapped roast duck. I just need to crisp it up and bone it for the shoot. I'm very comfortable boning ducks now after doing dozens. It's different than chickens. I'm confident with my knife skills. With over five years in New York kitchens and a childhood in my mom's kitchen I have plenty of calluses and scars to prove it.

I'm familiar with a lot of the kitchen equipment as well – Cuisinart's, mandolins, chinoises. But super-hot salamanders, pressure steamers, and kettles were new to me when I started here. Monster-size Hobart machines with attachments that do everything from kneading bread to whipping cream to pushing out sausage. There's much to learn and every new machine or tool I see brings to mind more possibilities. It allows me to play with the ordinary in hopes to turn it into the extraordinary.

I don't know what it is, but whenever someone says you must do it this way or that way, even in school, I would immediately ask… why? And look for another way it could be done, different, better. I don't know, call it anti-authoritarian or rebellious or something, but this place proved it to me. This was far from the traditional French cookbooks I flipped through back home.

But I'm comfortable, confident, and now, well... a professional. I'm in my checkered chef's pants and coat and I'm on my way to better things. I imitate my Mom and jump right in, blending ingredients artistically, tastefully, comfortably. I multitask, like her and my grandmother, working the ovens, sautéing, steaming, and grilling. By the end of the day I've completed six distinct plates: two entrees, two appetizers, and the two desserts, that were sent ready, I just had to garnish them, one with lemon zest, mint and fresh berries and the other with a chocolate lace and Chantilly cream.

Lionel's just caught them all on film and now he's sampling the roast duck with green peppercorn sauce. "This duck is awesome.... love the sauce, mmm and the skin cracklings."

"It's all the chef, man. His ideas, his creations."

"Yeah, but you execute it, bro. You're the last one with his hands on it before it goes public. That's no prepping potatoes"

"Yeah, I guess so. But the chef is the man, he's great, I'm really lucky to work so close with him." I feel proud, mission accomplished. I did it and I'm sure the chef will be happy with the results.

"That you are my man, that you are."

"You know, I'm gonna show my mom how to prepare this duck. She thinks it's always fatty."

Carving a duck is not carving a chicken. We partially bone it for this presentation. The leg and boned thigh is overlapped by the breast with part of the wing and interlocked neatly.

This restaurant makes eating easy for the guest. We slice their meats, remove cooked fish from the bone, and shell the lobster or crab. Even the accompaniments we serve are to make the dining experience easier. Fork to mouth, knife use is limited to steaks and chops.

The duck is served with herbed wild rice, pignoli nuts, and julienne of leek with chanterelle mushrooms sautéed in butter and finished with a bit of cream, salt, and white pepper. The bright golden mushrooms contrast with the shades of brown from the rice and duck. Lionel pierces a forkful of the wild mushrooms.

"Goooood. Mmmm, tastes as great as it looks." He lowers his eyelids savoring it, smiling. We move over and he focuses on the lamb, he loves tasting time.

"Chef went over and over this one with me. After I roasted it, I brushed a thin layer of green mustard across the top. Then pressed an herb blend of parsley, chives and mint into it and finish it by floating pink peppercorn flakes onto it.

Lionel looks down at the plate. "It looks cool, stuffed, different. The camera easily picked up the texture and colors. Very nice. They're gonna love it."

"Let me heat it up."

"Naaah, don't bother."

He picks up a chop from the sliced rack that's leaning with others against the risotto. It's medium rare with a perfect circle of spinach and mint centered in each chop. He drags it through the lamb demi-glace on the plate and in one bite, it's off the bone.

A large spoon of the risotto is centered on the plate; its rich orange butternut appearance is speckled with chopped sage and topped with two fresh sage leaves. A roasted blend of root vegetables, parsnip, celery root, carrots, and rutabaga tossed with chives forms a semi-circle around the top half of the plate. Lionel dips into the risotto with a fork and as soon as it hits his mouth his eyes roll.

"Awesome." he says, mouth full, savoring and slowly chewing.

"Everything at this restaurant kicks ass, bro," I say.

"That's the word around town."

He grabs another chop while swallowing the first, making sure it doesn't get away.

"Okay, I guess that's a wrap. Let's clean it up and call it a day, smoke a doob," I say as he stabs a forkful of roasted vegetables.

"Yeah, sounds good. Hey Chaz's brother is working the door at the Cannibal Club tonight, right?" Lionel asks.

"Yeah, he said we're cool, we're in… curious, never been."

"Yeah, me either. You sure we're in for free, bro? That's a tight club."

"Yeah, I think, but free or not, we're in. He said go right up to the front, we're on the list." It's impossible to get in this place otherwise.

"Okay, sounds good."

"Once you're in, Chaz said head down to the 'Caves'. There's always a party down there. I'll meet you there around eleven I'm going over to Debbie's for dinner, hang out a bit. She's on an early flight tomorrow and will be out of town for a few days."

I pull out a small joint from my toolbox I rolled earlier. "Let's go blow this really quick and wrap up after."

"Yes chef, sounds good."

"Don't call me chef, dude."

We step out into the sunlight and take seats on milk crates behind the cover of a dumpster. A stray dog appears behind it and scares the hell out of me by snarling. Lionel jumps back up towards the door. I put the joint in my mouth and with two hands grab a milk crate holding it up.

"Careful Nick that thing will bite you dude."

"Yeah, well, you got to show them who's boss." I tell him.

It growls, then barks as I toss the crate right at it, hoping to scare it away. The dog dodges the crate, baring its teeth. It looks right at me and starts barking loudly; *What the hell could it want?*

"Let's just blow this bone later, after we pack up," Lionel says.

"No, no dude. Just wait." I throw another. It barks louder.

"That dog looks like he wants a piece of you brother."

I kick another crate towards it and it finally turns, walking slowly away with its eyes on me still. Strange. Finally, … I can light this joint in peace.

✳✳✳✳✳✳✳✳✳✳

I stop and pick up condoms on the way to Debbie's. I hate them. Debbie insists I use them because there's a new disease out here now that's killing people. Nobody knows much about it, but all I know, is it takes me a lot longer to peak. Never had that problem with Gina. Especially after she started taking the pill less than a year ago. Never thought there'd be multiple partners. I remember Dad telling me that was the way it was meant to be, 'Just find one good one, that's all you need son.' he said. It may have worked back then, but it's a lot different now.

Gina and I had a routine down. And it was never one sided. Maybe that's what it is. I just need to get into a routine with Debbie. Although she seems to have one down already, she's having no problems. In fact, the squealing, squirming, and shaking is a bit scary at times.

She said she's cooking Mexican for dinner. Not my thing at all. Never saw it much back East. And when I did, it was restricted to chili and tacos. But out here, corn or flour tortillas are a staple, like white bread. Also, salsa, jalapeños and fresh avocado seem to cross all cultures out here, and, I've heard, are in every household in southern Cali.

I'd watch the prep guys when they cooked for themselves and for their amigos washing pots. And I've learned a lot. For one thing, more Spanish language than I ever learned in high school. Another

124

is that they didn't learn these dishes in college cookbooks and that's an advantage I can use.

Many start as pot washers and move up the line to prepping vegetables and eventually meat and fish. The chef gets in produce and ingredients just for them. Some are pretty good cooks, when they stick to their traditional dishes. I've seen plantains, banana, cooked several different ways. There's *yucca*, a root that I've never even seen in the markets back east before. And there are so many chili peppers I never knew existed.

Debbie's familiar with Mexican food. Tonight, she prepared some fresh fish tacos that the guys at work would have fought over. She's good in the kitchen and uses a lot of color.

She's been a bit spaced lately though, talking to me about some spiritual New Age stuff. It's a little freaky, and the music really sucks, just instruments, chimes, flutes and crap. She plays it at times when we're having sex. At least that makes it bearable.

The image of her naked is stuck in my head as I leave her place for the club. A picture of her newly shaved clean pubes is clearly in my mind. That was a surprise to me. Weird, never saw that in real life before and maybe only in one or two of my skin mags for that matter. It just doesn't look right, like she hasn't matured down there yet…kinda sick.

I park about a block away from the club and cut down an alley that leads to the street near the entrance. I just got paid and I'm looking forward to a good buzz, feed my head. In the alley, I hear something rustle by the trash bags. I look and suddenly see a shadow flash on the building wall. Well that's strange. Then I hear a bottle like it was kicked and now spinning. The alley's pretty dark, but an even darker image creeps by again. I walk faster, not interested in whatever's here, probably just a cat or some homeless guy.

And then suddenly to my right, a shadow appears in a doorway. The silhouette seems much bigger than a cat and it's too close for comfort.

My heart is racing and my legs pump and run like they haven't in years. Over my shoulder I see it falling behind as it pursues me. This is friggin eerie, and I want to get as far from it as possible, just get somewhere it will leave me be.

I run through the alley and into the streetlight and head towards the crowd in front of the club. I turn and it's nowhere to be seen. It's just suddenly disappeared. I stop for a moment to catch my breath and am relieved it's gone whatever it was. I need a drink.

I walk right into a crowd of pink and blue hair, hot pants, leather and chains, nose piercings, tattoos, and Mohawk haircuts spiked high. A huge mix of people waiting to be picked to get in, I push through to the small line where a bouncer is checking a guest list. Another huge bald-headed bouncer stands next to some guy I'm assuming is an owner or manager. He's picking out people from the crowd one at a time. Mostly hot girls and weirdos; there're plenty to choose from.

The guy checking the list allows people in by unhooking a thick red velvet cord from a post. He steps back as they slip through the stanchions and another bouncer opens the door for them. I'm next and I look up at the dude with the list.

"Last name."

"Anselmo, Nick."

"Right this way, sir," he says after briefly scanning the paper. He unclips the velvet cord and takes a step back.

I glance at the crowd and realize most of these people, especially the dudes, aren't getting in here. I step through the door and a fine-looking blonde girl in a tight leopard-skin body suit stamps the back of my hand.

"Welcome to the Cannibal Club. Your cover charge has been comped. Cheers!"

"Hey, thanks, cheers." I guess once you're on the list you're covered. I just saved twenty bucks. I look at the circle of ink fresh on the back of my hand, it's a skull. I feel really cool, like a VIP with celebrity access or something.

Wandering into the lobby I pass the cashier and a couple of cute coat-check girls standing in a big closet. My ears lead me to the music through the doorway on the other side. In the hallway, I'm stimulated with blacklights and visuals of skeletons hanging; skulls on posts, shrunken heads and bones glowing brightly down a long black stretch of corridor. Neon graffiti of crude prehistoric-type drawings of cavemen pursuing women and tangled in various sex positions.

Other sketches are of people dancing or clubbing one another. Bison, beasts, saber-tooth tigers and wooly mammoths add to the theme and glow all along the hall. Realistic rubber bats, spiders, and voodoo dolls are hanging from the ceiling, glowing neon green and orange. It's totally awesome, never seen anything like it, and I'm thrilled. It's like the biggest Halloween party times five thousand. I imagine if Gina was here she'd think this was pretty cool, I'm sure.

People are coming, going, squeezing their way around me, but I'm totally drawn to checking out the decor and lights. I'm wide-eyed, like a tourist. I reach and tap my pocket, making sure my cash is there, cause I'm heading right for the bar.

I exit the hallway into a jungle-like atmosphere of fog machines, darkness, colored lights, and weird characters. Immediately, I see life-size cages suspended by thick chains from the ceiling, like something out of a Frankenstein movie, with two beautiful chicks wearing leather and leopard-skin string bikinis. It's like they were just walked out of the movie 'Caveman' – a comedy with Ringo Starr that

Gina and I saw back in May. Each one has a bone clipped into their crazy-looking big hair and they dance wildly in the cages to the live band. No way could I take Gina here, just got a bit too weird for her.

Two shiny black guys are wearing leopard G-strings high on the platforms at each end of the long oval bar. The band is playing AC/DC, "Highway to Hell." My head can't help but move to the beat, and the rest of my body is vibrating from the thunderous bass.

I see two pierced punk chicks sandwiching a tattooed shirtless guy on the dance floor while surrounded by people grinding and humping upright. I mean I've seen some crazy dancing with disco, but this sure as hell isn't no disco.

I head over to the bar where people are four or five deep. Some are two-fisting beers, heads tipped back guzzling one right after another, like in competition or something.

Pushing through people I stop a few feet away from two guys who are racing down a pitcher each. A group circles them, chanting, some banging the bar with their fists like monkeys. This whole place so far seems dark, unruly, and I like it.

Chaz told me there's this huge heavyset guy that sits up in a balcony overlooking the dance floor and beautiful girls always surround him. He's a movie producer or something. This guy gets served hand over fist while supplying the club's guests with whatever drug they need. He has runners selling them throughout the club, Chaz said. Anything you could want is here.

I look up and around and sure enough there he is, on a big balcony in a huge chair with chicks all around him. Must be wannabes, because he has three unshaven chins, is seriously balding and slits for eyes. *Jabba the Hutt* comes to mind. It's crazy and exciting at the same time. I put a twenty-dollar bill up in the air and wave it over the head of the guy in front of me, I immediately get the bartender's attention, screaming my order over the band. "Long island iced tea!" he nods as he pours a row of drinks.

The dance floor is packed, and I see there's a scuffle between two really hot girls on the edge of it. I would bet both were the prettiest in their schools, if not their whole town. It's like LA has attracted the prettiest girls from every town in every nation, on a dream that Hollywood sold them. I mean, I've never seen so many beautiful girls in one place. One girl in the scuffle screams as she gets scratched by the other across the face. The scream pierces the air waves and sounds straight out of a horror movie. Heads turn as the other girl swipes back with nails out, before both entangle in a full force catfight.

"Iced tea." I hear.

It's perfect. Strong. Every white liquor in the rack. Tequila, rum, vodka, gin, triple sec, and a splash of coke for color. He hands me back eight bucks from the twenty and I leave a dollar on the bar. I knew they'd cost more here, but twelve bucks? It'll be a good attitude adjuster and I'll be feeling it in no time.

I turn to watch the girl fight, but it's been broken up. Both girls are a bit tattered and the boyfriend of one is trying to calm her down. It's very entertaining here and there's so much to see. Little scenarios going on everywhere, I feel I've been missing something for every night in my life that I haven't been here.

To the left on the dance floor is this shirtless guy with a tall orange spiked Mohawk gelled up tall like a rooster. He's like a punk rocker with six pack abs and solid muscles; but he's wearing a G-string and packing a zucchini in it.

Man, I'm sooo late. Lionel must be wondering where the hell I am.

I raise my voice to ask this Goth-looking girl next to me if she knows where the 'Caves' are. Her thick eye shadow, black lipstick, dark clothes, and piercings do nothing to reduce her allure. I wonder for a moment what makes her tick or turns her on. I notice her charcoal hair has blonde roots before her crystal blue eyes mesmerize me for a moment. She points with a black-lace fingerless gloved hand and I follow it with my eyes across the dance floor and see a circular stone opening framed by palms and potted plants lit up by large tiki torches. I'm sure I would have found it. It looks just like a cave opening. A deep red glow pulsates from the entrance and shadowy creature silhouettes are twisting on the inner hall.

I turn to thank her just as her friend returns, looking like a tall walking big black cat. She hands my mystery girl a drink, she raises it to me and smiles. Not sure what started this Goth stuff, but it's intriguing. I raise my drink to her and yell. *Gotta go. I'll be back.* I reluctantly leave with a smile. I'll go get Lionel and see if they want to smoke a joint. But I gotta find him first.

I head to the outskirts of the dance floor, but before making my way through the people with my drink, I turn to see the girls, get my bearings straight so I can make my way back. They're making out. I stare for a moment, *cool*.

I duck into the men's room to the left of The Cave to pee. I walk into the mob in the bathroom and some dude speaks to me.

"You want anything, I got joints, mushrooms, coke…," he says.

"No, I'm set."

"…acid, ludes, mescaline." He whispers.

"No, I'm good." I say again.

And I am. Lionel has some weed and I have some coke from Debbie. I wait my turn for a urinal or free stall. It's obvious by the deals going down and the multiple people in stalls that this bathroom isn't just for pissing. It's packed with smoke and people pushing stuff. An attendant offers hand towels after people wash their hands, and also combs, condoms, Polo and rolling papers with an array of toiletries.

There was an attendant at my cousin's wedding but you sure

couldn't get a whiff of glue or 'nitrous' for a dollar. I stay away from that crap. They say those inhalants instantly kill more cells in your brain than anything else, for a buzz that doesn't last.

Finally, a free urinal. I'm practically stampeded by three dudes that just left a stall cracking up hysterically. An older Spanish man rises from a stool and turns on the water as I approach the sink. I wash my hands and check out all the goods on the counter: cologne, loose cigarettes, gum, certs, Visine, papers, and lighters.

"See anything you need, boss."

"Not now, maybe later. Thanks."

I enter the glowing opening to the Caves, leaving the club lights behind as the music fades with every step I take down this descending torch-lit passageway.

Within a minute, I'm at a wide set of steps looking down at a large circular, dark, smoky lounge area. Like a sunken living room. Its backdrop has several torches lined around stonewalls and is spotted with palms. On low-lying sofas people are making out, smoking weed, snorting coke, and who knows what else off coffee tables. The live band has faded into the background upstairs. I can now hear laughter and conversation in my new surroundings. I look around the perimeter and there are several smaller connected rooms labeled 'Caverns.' They surround the common area, are secluded, darker and private.

I step down carpeted stairs holding a brass handrail into a darker lounge area. Within a minute, my eyes adjust to the lighting. I'm stunned when I suddenly see Lionel. He's right in the middle of two gorgeous women on a sofa. Arms around both of them, his grin is priceless, dreamlike. Lionel is not very suave with women, his words. *Maybe they're hookers?*

"Hey, hey Nick! Right here, over here man," he says waving me over. Within moments I'm stepping into their company. "Where you been dude? Sit down, sit down my brother, now here's my man Nick that I told you about."

"Nick... meet Monique." She lifts her hand to me; it's soft, smooth. Her smile intrigues. Her long black hair and cinnamon skin tone are special to me. Deep dark almond eyes and make-up remind me a lot of Cher, or Cleopatra. Glamorous.

"Hey….ehem, Hi Monique." She's no prostitute…I hope.

"And this is... is …uh" – he stutters while snapping his fingers.

"Tina, my name's Tina. And you're the 'Nick' your friend was talking about. He wasn't kidding, you look like *the man* all right." Not sure what she means but I'll take it as a compliment.

"Hi Tina. Hey, nice to meet you." Extending my hand to her as she looks me up and down, with a cute tight smile. Her short skintight dress, clings to her fine shape as she leans towards me revealing long shapely legs.

"Well, hello young man...Nicholas." She's pale in comparison to Monique, a cream-colored complexion. Long wavy strawberry blonde hair, seems soft, fitting her sparkling green eyes. They're both in their mid-twenties I'm pretty sure.

"Just 'Nick' is fine, Tina. Hey bro…I'm really sorry I ran so late."

"You're here that's all that matters, Nicholas."

"Really, just Nick's fine."

"So, what do you drive?" Tina asks.

What the..? "I just ran late getting out of the house. Not my car."

"Yeah but whatcha driving?" She insists.

She's no Valley Girl, I can tell by the tone of her voice.

"A Fiat X1/9. Why?"

"A Fiat? Do you know what Fiat stands for?"

"No…not really… What it stands for?."

"Fix It Again… Tony!" She says laughing.

I get it. Italian car company, a history of issues. I smile.

"Yeah, okay, good one."

"Get it, Nicholas? Fix.. It…"

"Yeah, yeah, I get, I get it. Fix it again Tony…Ha, heh, yeah!"

I don't like this one. Her laugh revealed gums two three times the size of her teeth. Plus, she's a wannabe Valley Girl, and that's just nuts. Monique's hotter, mysterious, and exotic-like.

"So, are we having a good time?" my eyes addressing Monique.

"Fabulous! Bitchin' band tonight."

"I know they're really cranking, right?"

A cocktail waitress approaches in a tiny black skirt, white skin-tight top, and a very sweet smile.

"You ladies like Kamikazes?" I ask. Not even sure if they heard of them. A popular shot back east vodka, lime juice, and triple sec or something.

"Love 'em," Tina says. Monique quickly nods in agreement.

"Cool. A pitcher of Kamikazes, and a Michelob, please."

The ladies stand, straighten their skirts and pick up their purses. Where the hell are they going? The party is just getting started.

"We'll be right back guys, need to use the ladies room." Tina says.

"Don't you two get lost now," Monique adds.

"Wouldn't think of it ladies," Lionel says.

He turns to me as they walk away, working it, as they round the corner.

"A couple of foxes, eh bro? We are in, dude." He beams a proud smile. "You gotta thank your friend, man, we would never have gotten in. This is like underground, secret, Hollyweird people."

"I know, right?" It's true. None of the normal dudes on that line are getting in.

This is really happening. I mean we're picking up chicks. And they're so hot!

"Hey they didn't ask you for money, right?"

"Nooo. No way man, they bought the first round."

"Really? Whoa…we're living the California dream, bro," I say.

"There's, like, no law here, if it feels good do it." I add, giddy about it.

"Free country bro… God bless America!"

Chapter Nine

Running with the Devil

"I got no love, no love you'd call real…"

~ Van Halen

FOR A FEW SECONDS, I hear the sound of a passing car or train horn and I know the next song the band is playing upstairs. The horn fades into a deep bass beat followed by a cymbal, then a twinkling of piano before it starts cranking out a song that's on my "Nick's mix" cassette. Van Halen's "Running with the Devil" is pushing the amps to the max.

I feel the crowds vibration as they pound the dance floor along with the sub-woofers.

Lionel taps me, and points to people doing coke off a small mirror on a cocktail table across the lounge. The smell of pot mingled with tobacco was already apparent in the room when I came in.

The waitress returns, setting the drinks down on the coffee table in front of Lionel and me.

"Here you go, gentlemen. That's forty-nine dollars."

I'm stunned. That's almost a day's pay. Five dime bags of pot, it's at least ten or twelve shots though. Lionel and I rummage in our pockets and put in thirty each.

"Keep it," I say.

"Thanks, I'll be in touch." Slipping it in her fanny pack as she saunters away.

I notice Monique and Tina approaching, arm in arm. They wear the highest, pointiest heels I've ever seen. I tap Lionel and tilt my head towards them. They seem close, a little closer than just friends. Lionel's focusing and he starts writhing in his seat and enthusiastically turns to me.

"Whoa…Nick. Ooh, oh man, we might see more action than I thought... I'm getting a stiffy."

As cool as Lionel is, he's a little awkward with the ladies, always has been he's told me.

"Chill, bro. Don't be a spaz," I say.

The girls lower back down into the sofa.

"So, you ladies wanna do a shot?" I pick up the pitcher of Kamikazes and start pouring.

"Hey, let's have a toast!" Tina says.

I hand a shot to each of the girls and Lionel.

Monique quickly raises the shot glass into the air and we all follow along.

"YES, yes, I say we toast to all the great vibes in this place and to future… nudity!"

She draws her shoulder back and shimmies, sending her breasts into a bouncing jiggle in her loose satin tank top. Lionel's eyes bug as she slowly licks her upper lip. He's a bit shaky as he lifts his glass higher, but his grin is sure and steady.

Yeah…she's definitely the cooler of the two. She handles herself in a way that's just outright sexy. It's like every move is worth watching. I could see myself hanging out with Monique. The age difference with Debbie is just awkward at times in public.

"Yeaaah, baby. I'll drink to that. Sweet!" Lionel says with a huge smile.

"Oh yeah, let's PARR-TEE!" I raise my glass in unison.

"Okay, boys, let's see those bottoms up!" Tina chimes in.

"Yes, boys. Bottoms up!" Monique echoes, chuckling. Yeah, definitely, I'm gonna ask her out to a movie. That's something I really miss doing with Gina.

They swallow the shots with practiced ease. Lionel grimacing from it, leans back, and pulls a joint out of his shirt pocket and turns to Tina.

"You wanna smoke a joint?" he asks.

She's sucking on another Marlboro Red, the third in quick succession.

"Absolutely." she says.

Tina pulls a Bic out of her purse as Monique pulls a fat joint out of her cleavage.

"You boys need to try some of this. Check it out. Got it from my amigos on the boulevard."

She pulls a plastic bag of pot from her purse and passes it to me. I open and get a whiff of it. It's sweet, intriguing, and strong. Its scent is like none I've ever smelled before.

"Whoa! Mmmm. Smells awesome."

"Feel it. Check out the buds…sticky, right? she says. See the purple and red hairs on it?"

I pick it up, smell it again and take a closer look, never seen anything like it. I pinch a bit between my fingers; it's moist, it does feel sticky.

I love herbs. I mean my profession is full of them. Although I can't imagine any culinary use for this off hand, my interest is piqued nonetheless. Monique lights it and passes it to me.

"A hundred and twenty bucks an ounce. I can get you a half-ounce for sixty-five. Barely any seeds, if you're interested."

Lionel passes his joint to Tina and she immediately places the lit end into her mouth and closes her lips around it; she leans into Lionel, gently pulling his neck and face closer and blows a stream of smoke through the joint right at a startled Lionel.

He catches on and sucks as much as he can of the stream until a plume of reefer smoke surrounds his face and head.

I exhale, looking over at Lionel and Tina as he goes into a slight coughing fit. I turn to Monique as the smoke of her weed passes out of my mouth and nose.

"Wow, smooth. Amazing."

I watch Tina toke on Lionel's joint and quickly makes a sour face, putting it down in the ashtray, then reaches for the one in my hand.

"Hey, Lionel, you should check this out. You want to split a half ounce?" I say.

I've never paid more than ten or twenty bucks for a bag of pot. Then again, I never bought anything like this. Tina hands the joint to Lionel.

"A few hits of that and your good for a while," she tells him.

I pour more Kamikazes and pass them around.

"Damn, bro. Mine tastes like dirt compared to this. Count me in," Lionel says.

"Yeah it is," Tina agrees.

Then Monique reaches in her purse and takes out a sandwich bag half full of cocaine. My eyes pop; it's the largest amount I've ever seen.

I quickly look around to see if anyone's watching. A joint or two or ten is one thing, but a bag of coke like that and you'll be doing time or could get killed for it.

Lionel sees the coke and his eyes bug; he coughs out some smoke as he looks around with serious concern.

"Relax, boys. Nobody's gonna bust us. We do this here all the time. We take care of the bouncers," Tina says.

Within seconds Monique dumps out ten times more coke onto the glass coffee table than I've ever seen on a mirror with Debbie. She begins to crush and chop it nonchalantly with the edge of a credit card.

I'm pretty impressed; not everyone has access to coke. It's expensive and having a lot seems to really just exist in rich and celebrity circles.

"Don't you just love MTV?" Monique asks as she chops a way. Music television, MTV is something they just launched last summer. Rock music synched with videos. Now it seems musicians can't seem to get a hit song without a good video.

She smiles, adding, "Isn't it just rad?"

"Yeah, *Video Killed the Radio Star…*"

Chapter Ten

Lola

"Girls will be boys and boys will be girls…"

~ Kinks

THE COVER BAND PLAYS ON an upstairs stage, but down here the sound of people pulling on joints, giggling, and moaning intermingles with the sound of cocaine being snorted. Monique cuts these large lines of blow, 'rails' she calls them. She leans down and inhales one up her nostril; it's gone in an instant. She evens it out with a second line up the other one, like a pro. She hands the cut plastic straw to Lionel.

"Here you go honey, have a blast."

Lionel's not much into coke, he likes his pot. He knows I have a tiny brown vial of coke in my pocket from Debbie— later in the night he may take a spoon or two. But Tina just snorted the amount of what I have in the vial already and there's five times that much on the table.

Taking the straw from her, his eyes on her chest, her nipples, pert in her blouse.

"Yeah sure thanks," he says as he leans down and inhales half a line. "Whoa… that's good, yeah." I can tell he's unsure, feeling the burn from it.

He leans down and inhales half of the other half. Grimacing, he hands me the straw. I pass it to Tina.

"No, you go ahead, enjoy." She smiles at me.

I do a bump once in a while with Debbie now. Or after work, here and there, when offered at the bar but I can't help thinking, free coke. Never know if I'll ever see this much again for free, this isn't cheap. I follow Tina's lead and lean into a line like a champ. In an instant, it disappears as my nostril feels the sting, and I lift my head back knowing already that this night will be like no other.

I lean down into a second one, inhaling most of it. Then I slide my finger over the rest and rub it into my gums like I've seen Debbie do. Within moments my gums and lips are numb. I pass the straw to Tina and she slides closer to take it. She places her other hand on my upper thigh. I'm feeling confident, exhilarated and numb.

"Lionel tells us you're a chef!" Tina says.

"Yeah well not quite, I'm working on it though."

"Don't let him fool ya. He's got it going on. My man from New York…he's a chef," Lionel says.

Monique holds her nose, sniffles, and turns to me.

"Is New York just like in the pictures? Ya know skyscrapers and everything?"

I can't seem to place her accent – it seems almost southern, or maybe western.

"Yeah, I guess. A bunch of tall buildings clustered together on an island. LA's definitely more spread out. I haven't seen a line of people anywhere other than the clubs and drive-thru's."

"I'd say. Been there. New York is tight. Like sardines, subways and lines of people walking everywhere. I mean nobody walks in LA," Lionel says.

"Yeah, but Broadway, the clubs, SoHo, and Greenwich Village. I dreamed of living there. I just had to get out of the little town where I grew up in Utah," Monique says.

"So, what do you cook? What's your specialty?' Tina asks.

I'm not sure how to answer that since I don't think I have one. But before I can answer, she keeps talking.

"Christmas is around the corner and I'm gonna miss my mom's green-bean casserole, again… I love the crispy onions on top. You know how to make that Nick, with the Campbell's mushroom soup?"

I have no idea what's she's talking about. But as soon as she says Campbell's, I don't really want to know. "No, can't say I do."

"You never had green-bean casserole? It's soooo good. My mom makes ambrosia every year too!" Monique chimes in.

I hate to ask. Part of me says I'm a professional and I'm supposed to know everything. But that sounds foreign, ya know, fancy to me. I'm curious.

"Ambrosia, what's that?"

"You're a cook and you don't know what that is?" Tina asks.

"It's got marshmallows, mandarin oranges, canned pineapple, cool whip and I think coconut and maraschino cherries, right Tina?" Monique says.

Gross. A bunch of cheap canned stuff, with marshmallows and fake whipped cream. "Wow... hey that sounds interesting," I say.

Monique licks her lips and I notice a tiny speck of coke on the tip of her nose.

"It's delicious. She makes an onion dip with Lipton soup mix. Mmmm... Oh, and Vienna sausages, and a big cheddar-cheese ball rolled in nuts for starters."

"Vienna sausage...what's that?" *Sounds Italian.* I reach over and gently wipe the coke off her nose with my thumb.

"Mmm..mm.. They are, deee-lish," Tina says, piquing my curiosity.

Monique nods. "Armour and Libby's makes them, ya know. They're like mini hot dogs that come in a little can. My mom fries them."

Now, is it a hot dog or a sausage? And it's sure not Italian if it's from Armour.

"Oh ehem... interesting." I say, as my eyes gravitate back to her chest.

I look over to Lionel and he shrugs his shoulders. He knows good food. He's seen a helluva-a-lot-more professional chefs at work than me in his career. I'm thinking, this is what we've been sold on in this country, Chef Boyardee, cans, and TV dinners? *Please make it stop.*

My mom went to the butcher's, fish markets, and the bakery. There're still a few local vegetable markets around us as well. We only went through the canned aisles at the supermarket occasionally for things we otherwise couldn't find fresh, olives, anchovies, oils, and stuff. But these girls seem to have had an upbringing in food closer to some of my friends back home, like at Pauly's house.

I'd love to tell Pauly about the stewardess and what's happening out here. Rub it in a little. He loves fantasizing about all the girls and stuff. Just what he always dreamed about. But I'm not sure I could trust him with this. He talks too much.

I may have my magazines, but I was always happy if it was just Gina and me. She blows away all the centerfolds in my mind. It was much more than just sex. But I admit who knew how fun a little variety could be? I'm surprised about how easy it is. But I can't run the risk of her finding out by talking to Pauly. I plan on getting together with her again. The spa plan is alive and well and I'm hoping this is just a break for a while to concentrate on it.

Her mom was a lot cooler when I just called to leave her my new number. I really hope she calls; it's been too long without talking. Maybe by spring break we can work this out.

That's months away and I'm sure she's very focused on school right now. I am happy she's going to the school she wanted to. We can still do this; I would have been apart upstate studying anyway.

I feel warm hands on my shoulders working their way down my biceps to my chest. Monique's head moves in next to mine from behind.

"Come on cutie, follow me," she whispers in my ear then gently squeezes it between her lips.

Electricity runs up my back and neck as my arms break out in goose bumps. I rise and follow in a sort of sexual stupor.

I look to Lionel and it seems Tina's taken Monique's cue and moved in closer to him. Her ivory hand is moving to his upper thigh. He glances at me and I give a nod, trying to be cool and hold back my smile, so I don't look as silly as he does with his.

Tina moves in on his neck, running a hand up the back of his 'fro as his eyelids gently shut. His smile opens and Tina slowly plants her lips on his. Can't say I've ever seen the salt and pepper contrast so up close.

Monique has a few years on me, but she's a beauty, in her mid-twenties, I think. She holds my hand, leading me towards one of the surrounding 'caverns.'

Only leopard skin curtains separate the private rooms around the common area. I'm not sure where this is going, but this just may be a home run.

From what I learned from Debbie, porn tapes, and the Penthouse Forum, older women seem more interested in having sex than the girls back in high school. My friends would say the girls in school just wanted to play with your head. These women want to play with all of you.

"No glove, no love," is the saying going around lately, so I always have one with me just in case because you're not getting lucky if you're getting an STD.

"What did you think of that blow?" Monique asks as she peeks through a curtain into a cavern to check if it's empty. It is, and we enter.

My heart is racing a bit, my jaw seems to be moving on its own and I can feel the coke residue from my nostrils seep down into my throat, which seems to numb everything on the way down.

"Yeah, I like it. That's good stuff."

She smooths her hand over my left ass cheek and squeezes it. *Wow.*

Something in me is hungry to reciprocate, but I'm unsure, nervous of what her reaction may be. But my hunger gets the better of me and I reach under her skirt and gently guide my hand over her panties, feeling her ass. I can't believe this is happening.

"Yeah… good stuff," she says softly.

In the dimly lit cavern she pulls me into her.

My hand moves up her torso under her loose blouse. My thumb and forefinger brush over her lacy bra, seeking out what has occupied my attention all night. Her other hand travels around front and starts touching me slowly over my jeans, I rise in response.

Her cinnamon- skin contrasts against mine as her dark-brown eyes and full lips lean into me, closer to where I feel her breath on my neck. My hand continues to explore her body, admiring her smooth, jet-black hair, down to mid back. I assume she's part Mexican or Indian.

With my hand under her blouse, I lower the top of her bra a bit and take a peek. Then I gently lead her down to the couch thinking, smooth, I got this.

At this point, the conversation is in body language. Monique alternates between rubbing my crotch and squeezing my chest. Her skirt rides up her thigh and her smooth legs are fit and long. I move my way up her toned arms, pulling her bra strap down over her shoulder, releasing her. I slowly fill my palm, gently smoothing my thumb over her. She slips my zipper down and moans as her hand holds onto me.

"Do you have a condom?" She says.

"Yeah." Nervously, I go to pull it out of my back pocket.

"Not yet, young man. We'll get to that. Just relax, let's take it nice and easy."

I'm past buzzing from the coke and drinks, I'm floating, not a worry in the world. She reaches down with her other hand and starts rubbing herself under her skirt.

My body responds effortlessly, naturally. I'll just let it have its way. I smooth my hand along her waist and she gently takes it, guiding me, as her almond eyes look straight into mine, captivating me. She licks her lips, smiling wide before placing my hand onto her silk panties, which feel strange, bulging and full. What the…?

I jolt up pushing her hard off me, she hits the floor. My heart drops to my stomach and I feel nauseous, an awful nervous fear rises in me and then morphs into rage.

"Shit! Oh, no… Oh shit." I bolt out of the cavern, shirt open, stumbling as I try zipping up my pants as I make my get away.

But Monique is right behind me with her skirt up to her waist and an obvious erection bulging in her panties. She grabs my arm and pulls me back to her.

"C'mon where we going, pretty boy? You haven't seen anything yet. So much to learn sweet cheeks." She then whispers into my ear, "I got some really good stuff to turn you onto." She then licks my ear.

"A whole new world to explore, it'll take you to the point of no return. Neverland and Pleasure Island, so many pretty boys you'll want to stay there forever." She whispers seductively.

I tear my arm loose from her grip, trembling, shocked and angry. "Get away man! You psyched me out. That's sick… bitch!" I push 'Monique' hard and he stumbles off spiked heels crashing to the floor. I turn to rush out, but he gets up, kicks off the shoes and comes at me in a rage. He grabs both of my arms firmly in one of his and then hits me, with a hard backhand. My head swings around twisting my neck.

"Oh… so you like it rough, huh, baby boy?" Her voice drops a couple of octaves. "And who you calling a bitch?" He grabs my arm again and kicks my feet out from under me sending me down hard onto the floor. Her hair falls off, a wig. She quickly kneels over me pinning me down.

People start crowding around, murmuring and talking.

"This boy bothering you, Monique?" somebody asks.

"Yeah… do we need to teach him a lesson?" Another woman steps in closer and says with a man's voice. "Oh my… he is a youngster. Yes… hmm. Chill girl. You may want to be gentle with this boy, he looks like a keeper, movie material." The deep raspy voice that comes out of this woman is just freaking me out.

"No I'm taking this. This is so hot. Watch the door." 'Monique' says, straddling my abs.

"You sure? Let me give him something to relax honey. Then we can take him home for an after party, maybe pitch him in San Fernando as a newbie."

My heart is racing like never before. *What the hell are they talking about?* I can taste blood in my mouth. That smack made me bite my tongue or something. I look up and see her short nappy haired head and I just yell out. Loud. "LIONEL! Hey Lionnnelll, help!"

'Monique's' face distorts with many mixed expressions, emotions, which end in a rage. She grabs one of her pointy heeled shoes.

"YOU! Hurt my feelings. H-how dare you offend me, a lady? Me…a LADY!" His eyes fill with tears and she begins weeping. Huffing, she lifts his stiletto shoe high above my face. My eye's cross trying to focus on the heel that's about to puncture my face.

"No… please no…'Monique'. My mistake. Big mistake!" I hold my hand up to block the heel.

Her face now unrecognizable, from the one I first saw.

I quickly cover my eyes and twist my body over to protect it. Within seconds someone starts pulling hard on my jeans, taking my underwear along with it. I struggle hard trying to turn, but someone else takes hold of my shoulders. I sense the air on my ass as my face is painfully pressed into the floor.

"Oh, that's sweet, yeesss. Sweet cheeks… mmhmm." she says and then slaps me there. The more I struggle the stronger their grip.

"Get the hell off me, man!" My body trembles, overcome with panic. My mind thinks I'm in an insane asylum or in a hardcore prison. *No..No. Please…this is not happening!*

"Please 'Monique', seriously, please!" I turn seeing her raging face with eyes, cold, black, desolate. I try to reach her through them pleading, "PLEASE…please... Don't hump me Bro..."

His soulless eyes glimmer in a sincere moment of connection, focusing on mine with a sudden concern. Man, that was close. Then just as quick they go blank. Dark again. He's not stopping.

"LIONEL!" I scream out louder. His large hand quickly covers my mouth tight, squishing my nose and making it hard to breath. My cheek is throbbing from the pain as blood builds in my mouth. People stand there, watching my assault with sick grins, blocking the view of anyone who might pass by. Like it's a fight in high school, but instead it's like some sick gang rape.

As my face is being pulled up from the floor, by his hand that's muffling my mouth, I see Lionel break through the ring of spectators.

"Nick! NICK! What the…" Lionel charges in and pushes 'Monique' off me, sending him sprawling onto the cavern floor. The one holding me just let's go and backs away so as not to be seen. The others quickly dissipate into the shadows. Show over.

Lionel pulls me up and we book it through the orange-lit hall, onto the dance floor and through the thick crowd of people as we head for the exit.

I'm off balance, stumbling, feeling sick, nervous, freaked out, and scared. And I can't seem to get out of there fast enough. The thought they might be following us hits me.

"I think... I think I'm gonna puke, dude."

"No way...c'mon, book it!" Lionel says, grabbing my wrist and pulling me through the tightly packed space. "Pleeaase move it, move it! Coming through, coming through, sick man about to hurl!"

Upon hearing this, people parted. Nobody wants warm chunks of puke spewed onto their Saturday-night threads. We break through to the outside and push through the crowded lines. We find a spot on the curb and lean against a couple of metal newspaper dispenser's.

"You okay, Nick?" Lionel says, breathing very heavy.

"I don't know man, that was screwed up. Dude… you saved me man," I say just as winded.

"No…you saved me, when I jumped up Tina's wig fell off. Man, I'm so stupid."

"Saved you? She didn't have you pinned, down."

My nausea subsides. I look up from the curb; I swear I see that damn dog again. Sniffing around further up the block. I squint, trying to focus, but in a flash, like a shadow it seems to disappear into the people passing on the sidewalk. I wonder if I'm just seeing things.

"Damn man, that turned freaky pretty quick." Lionel says, as I spit blood into the sewer.

"That's for sure." Pauly is never gonna hear about this. Never, ever, ever.

Chapter Eleven

Fire and Rain

"Just yesterday morning, they let me know you were gone…"

~ James Taylor

No idea how long the phone's been ringing, but I heard the last four rings. I squint towards the alarm clock. 3 AM? Wrestling my arms out of the sheets, I knock a full ashtray onto the floor reaching for the phone. I continue past beer bottles and the *Hustler* mag on my nightstand to pick the phone up. *Who the hell is calling me this late?* I wonder if Lionel got home all right. It's only been a couple of hours since we left the club.

"Hehmm…Yeah.".

"Nick?" Familiar voice.

"Yeah…he hem."

"I know it's early out in L.A. I'm sorry... but… I got some bad news." It's Pauly.

"Pauly? Hey, wha…what's up dude?"

"Gina was in a car accident last night Nick."

"Oh no, man…how's she doing." The news works its way slowly into my brain.

"Well, not so good dude."

"Oh, umm, so what hospital is she in?" I'm nervous about the "news" she must be hurt.

There's no answer.

"Which hospital Pauly?"

"She didn't make it Nick." His voice cracks. "She…she died."

He sounds serious. *He is serious.* My mind becomes numb, blank. My chest tightens with pressure as my body sits stunned. My insides become filled with a torrent of pain, that's far from physical. The same pain inside when I saw my Dad die. Instinctively my eyes squeeze shut as I try to connect my mind with what he just said

157

and not re-live the pain from my past. My head's rejecting what he just said, because it may just be a bad dream. Yeah…yeah… I get them sometimes.

Moving slowly while sitting upright on the edge of the bed I place my feet flat on the floor. Just wake up. I scratch my head, quickly rub my face which makes me wince; reminding me my face was pressed into the club floor last night. I drop my forehead into my hand as my elbows rest on my knees.

"Nick?" I hear my name.

"Hey, Nick!" yells Pauly, my silent moment of uncertainty has passed back into reality.

"Nooo… No way Pauly. No way, how do you know?"

"I'm serious Nick. I'm sorry to tell you this man. Nobody here even knows yet. It's six in the morning and only a few people at the diner heard about it last night."

"A car accident? Wha…what h-happened?' My tongue feels swollen in my mouth. I can't speak properly as my voice suddenly cracks.

"I don't think you know this and I didn't want to be the one to tell you, but she started hanging out with Patsy quite a bit. She started partying."

"Patsy? C'mon man… Patsy? My head throbs despite my holding it. "What do you mean, "partying?"

"Who knows, I mean, she was a little freaked when you split. We were a bit worried. She changed, cut and dyed her hair and stuff. She became a little punk and started hangin' with Patsy. The word is that they weren't going out, just hanging out." He quickly adds.

"She dyed her hair? Punk? Hangin' with Patsy? Hey Pauly, I tried reaching her, but she hasn't returned my calls." It pierces my mind; I will never see her again. "She broke up with me man. I didn't freak her out." My heart sinks at the thought of the last day I saw her.

"Whatever, Nick. But she had a hard time after starting school downtown."

"I'm telling you she broke up with me man! I wanted her out here but she didn't want to come. Damn— this isn't my fault," I say as my fist hits the wall. I kick the fallen ashtray across the floor and quickly rummage through my drawer for a cigarette. My hands tremble as the pain in my knuckles throbs.

"Hey, take it easy Nick. Chill. Nobody said it's your fault. It's an accident man, they happen."

"Well, what the hell happened?" I open the Marlboro Lights and pull a smoke out with my lips.

"Phil was at the club. He said Patsy ate three Quaaludes that he knew about there, before they left the Ritz. He didn't think anything of it, 'cos Patsy's been handling up to six ludes just fine nowadays."

It looks like he passed out or something, because he veered into an oncoming lane and into another car. It was a pretty bad scene. A young lady and her boy didn't make it either. Gina died instantly Nick…she never knew what hit her."

"Where's Patsy?" I light the cigarette, inhaling a big drag.

"He's in the hospital, broken ribs, concussion. He's in for a couple of nights of tests."

"I just can't see her getting in Patsy's creepy car." I exhale streams of smoke through my nostrils. "Patsy should've friggin' died." Mr. Cinelli clearly comes to mind. "Did you see her parents?"

"They're devastated Nick. I heard through Lisa that her mom was in shock at the hospital. Says 'She's in God's hands now'. Lisa says they're both lost, out of it. She's really freaking out they were real close lately. We're all blown away…can't believe it."

"Her mom, oh man, God's hands? Yeah… right. Even after this? There's no God, Pauly. Never was. I gotta go tell Chaz. I'll call you later."

"Wait…wait, Nick. That's not all. Damn, man… I don't talk to you for months and now…um, I feel like I gotta tell you this. She was pregnant Nick, when you left. I had no idea. No one did, only Lisa."

WHAT? I wish I never answered this phone… If I just let it ring, then everything would be okay. I look through the ashes on the floor for a roach or a half of joint to light.

"Damn Pauly how long did you know this?" Unreal…unreal I can't believe it.

"Lisa just told me last night, after the accident."

"Yeah…well, WHAT?"

"She said… well, her and Gina went to the clinic for an abortion a couple of months ago." My hand begins to tremble as I try to light the roach, balancing the phone between my shoulder and ear.

"Yeah…Yeah.. and?

"Well, Lisa said Gina was shaking so much…she couldn't go through with it. She was glad to leave that place and was going to tell her parents, and you, when the time was right." I give up on the roach, throwing it across the room.

"If the hospital confirms she was pregnant, her parents are gonna know. Patsy was so high, he's sure to be doing time. I'm sorry to bring this news, bro, really, I can't tell you how bad this sucks. When you flying home…?"

My hands begin to tremble again, then my arms, torso, and legs. I feel no pain from the night before, just a knotted up heavy weight in my chest and head, as I try in vain to stop myself from shaking. My knees weaken, and I sink to the floor still holding my phone to my ear. There's no way I'm going back and facing her father.

"Home…uh…yeah, uh, home, I don't think so. I just got a promotion and it's real busy out here, I could lose my job." I feel numb, drained.

"Nick…seriously?"

"Damn Pauly, I can't face her family man, her dad. I can't believe she was pregnant. Man, I'm freakin' out here, I gotta go tell Chaz." I slowly get up.

"Yeah, I hear ya, Nick. But it's Gina. You should think about it and tell Chaz I'm sorry. I really am so sorry, Nick."

"She told me she wasn't pregnant man, she told me…she told me."

I hang up the phone with my head spinning. I'm numb as I walk down the hall. Last night fades so far from me now. An overwhelming feeling of anger rises up in me and I want to kill Patsy, literally. I think about flying back there and kicking his ass right in the hospital and choking him to death.

Taking a breath, I open Chaz's door, not sure how to tell him about Gina without choking up or breaking down in tears. I see through the dimly lit room Chaz, with a shocked look on his face. Taking a step in, my eyes adjust to the darkness, and I quickly step back through the door into the hall. My shaking stops suddenly as I see Chaz and another guy, naked, thigh over thigh on his couch. I've met the guy here before, his 'friend', older guy. I try but fail to get out a few words. I turn my head away as my stomach starts to twist and wrench. And last night comes rushing back into my mind.

"Oh, come on...What the… damn, dude!" shoots out of my mouth.

Instinctively I turn my head as my stomach begins to heave, I hurry my pace as it convulses. I bolt out the back door, in my underwear, and spew puke behind a hedge off the back step. The image of what they're doing sends my head spinning.

That type of sex life never entered my mind. My nude mags were so far from that. Disturbing to see. Baffling.

My mind's overloaded and my stomach's still queasy, but I gotta get out of the house. I head to my room. Chaz is walking through the hallway towards me tying his robe. He motions for me to stop. I do, standing in my underwear, uncomfortably, a first with him.

161

"Nick…Nick…listen man. I've wondered about this for a while."

"Not now man…just…just, not now." I say, he looks at me nervously.

"Nick, please…you'd be amazed at how many guys are bi" I turn my head to the ground.

"If it feels good…do it, right? Well I'm not feeling it. So just, accept it."

"Hey, it's not as strange as you may think. So many peop…".

"SHUT UP!" I take a breath... and look him square in the eye.

"Gina's dead… call Pauly." I slam my door so I can get dressed.

Never felt so sure about getting away from here. Just jumping in my car and driving away, far away, aimlessly. Which I immediately do.

At a Seven- Eleven I buy smokes and a Bud Tall Boy. I lean back in my bucket seat, light a smoke, and sip the beer. I just gaze up at the dark night sky as the cigarette smoke rises above my roof, like a cloud, blocking out the stars.

I peel out of the parking lot and it's not long before I hit Pacific Coast Highway with an ocean of black right in front of me, just past the sand. For a moment, I wish I could drive right into it, disappear into the blackness.

I light a joint and turn south towards San Diego. Start feeding my head, a needed morning buzz. Alternating between toking on the joint and sipping my beer. And begin to feel better already.

My headlights cut through to the blacktop ahead as I punch it out and turn on my car stereo to play something loud. Instead, James Taylors, *Fire and Rain*, has just begun. I usually change the station for something mellow like this, but for some reason, the still of the night, the calm empty road ahead, I listen intently for the first time. His lyrics hit me. I hear them like I never did before. The realization that I'll never see Gina again chokes me. My eyes moisten into fast tears falling.

I read in Rolling Stone that this song had to do with a girl he knew who committed suicide, as well as his issues with addiction, heroin. Why it seems so relevant to Gina right now I don't know. But man, the sixties could get deep.

Did I forget how quick life could be taken, especially after my Dad's death? Suddenly I want to see my Mom, my family. Who's next? What if I don't see them again?

In less than an hour I'm pulling off PCH onto Beach Boulevard in Orange County. I take it to the pier in Huntington Beach. I light a large roach from my ashtray, to be sure I stay high. Looking out over the ocean as that song, long gone, plays over and over in my head.

Surfers in wet suits sit on the beach. I assume they're waiting for daybreak before they hit the surf. Fishermen walk past me onto the pier with big plastic buckets and their tackle. The tempo of the morning slows down to the peaceful rhythm of the waves breaking on the shore. I'm getting tired, I take out the vile of coke.

It was tough moving out of Chaz's while he's in school, not saying a word. But between the club scene, Gina's death, and walking in on him, I just can't face him. Not yet. Debbie bought a bathrobe with my initials monogrammed on it. She's excited I'm moving into her townhouse. Me? Not so much.

****

Sunny Days That I Thought Would Never End....

~ James Taylor

The sting of Gina's death can only be numbed by more drinks, drugs, and jumping head first into working extra hours. I'll take as much work as they'll give me. More photo shoots, catered events, and longer shifts increase the demand for more cocaine. I need to stay busy. Busy is good, virtuous…*right*?

Take a second job and there's no time to think about everything. I run to three locations at a time. The photo shoots are a bit off-season so I see Lionel a lot less lately. We'd hook up if I wasn't so booked between catering, my job at the restaurant, and an easy late night gig cooking a room service menu at Le Mondrian hotel on Sunset Boulevard. It's never too busy that late, so I get to relax a bit.

Every kitchen job in LA comes not just with a variety of good food, but booze, women, and coke. It's only been close to a year since I left New York. I have a lot to learn still, many questions, but I seem to be giving more and more directions to the new guys now.

The fun's beginning to fade, the kitchens are busy as hell and the chefs are always demanding long hours. They feed your pride with a higher position, which means more responsibility, and give you a chef's coat with your name on it for compensation. Then they suck enough life from you to kill three people. They move one up then let go of two; happens all the time.

I'm tired of seeing the not so thick-skinned guys from school getting chewed up, spat out within a couple of months, then move on to some office job far away from the cutting boards and stove just so they can pay their loan. The competition, professional jealousies and huge egos are way too much for most. Putting a bunch of artists in a closed area with fire, knives, and frying pans doesn't always work out so well

Stress, cuts, pressure, blisters, and burns always come with the sweat and tears. It's part of the daily grind under some of the head chefs. And they have their own pressures. I learned that chefs rarely look at a long bright future at any one place. Especially since the 'personnel' department disappeared and became 'Human Resources.'

Something about those words doesn't sit well in my head. But even knowing how it is, I buy into it like all the chefs before me who lived to work, instead of working to live. Gotta pay the bills, right?

I realized today it's about sixth months since I got that call from Pauly. I've been too busy to stay connected back East…got a lot going on out here.

The constant rays of the California sun highlight the pollution in such a way that makes the smog seem impenetrable, when looking down over it from Hollywood Hills it's quite obvious. It's a poisonous blanket that covers the whole city and slowly chokes the people within it. But just driving down Sunset Boulevard in the middle of it, you wouldn't even know you're being tainted, infected.

I walk past the garbage dumpster, boxes, crates, and grease barrels and into the back door of the kitchen. Glad to be out of the heat and smog of the city.

The noise of exhaust fans, clanging of pots, and dishes have become the norm now for the majority of my days. Smoked duck is in the air and as I pass the pastry kitchen my nose picks up poached pears and caramel as well.

I turn the corner and there's Manuel, one of the busboys. Just the guy I wanted to see.

"Hey boss! I was chust..lookin' for chu mon." He motions me into the storeroom.

"We cool?" I ask.

"Yeah… yeah, sure boss." He hands me a folded magazine paper half the size of a Sweet and Low packet, four times as fat.

I slip him five twenties. *It's my third gram in the last two weeks. This'll last a few days, get me past this second straight week of work.*

"Very cool, thanks, Manny."

"Any time, boss. Any time. Ya need to take care of the cook if chu wanna eat good, right?"

"Yeah sure, Manny. Swing by after rush hour I'll hook you up."

A gram's usually a hundred and twenty bucks, Manuel sells it cheaper. He never disappoints. The "go-to" guy for everyone in this place and some of the bar clientele as well.

I wouldn't need to buy it this often, but Debbie's been flying for weeks. She's stopping in Miami and will be back with a quite a bit of blow. Won't cost me a dime then.

Coke's been a necessity lately due to a never-ending work week. Every day is a Monday. I wipe down the back of the toilet and lay out a line. Any stall in the staff bathroom is a common spot for this throughout the night. I hear someone enter the bathroom. I stay quiet, hesitate, and wait to inhale the line.

"Hey Nick? Hey let me get a blast?" It's Brandon, one of the waiters. His lisp is a dead giveaway.

"Sure Brandon, no problem… hold on." I spill out more and chop up a line for him. "I know something you don't know." He's an openly gay waiter, and a notorious gossip.

"Oh yeah, what's that?" I ask through the stall door.

"You know Dina, that pretty little hostess?"

"Yeah. The cute brunette. The one that looks like Barbi Benton?" I lean into the line on the toilet.

"Yup! That one. She likes you sweet cheeks. And she loves to party." He's quite the matchmaker, he believes.

"No kidding? A bit outta my league don'cha think?" I stand upright, pinching my nostrils. "She's probably seeing someone…no?"

I slip out of the stall and hand the straw to Brandon.

"She may be, but I bet it's not serious," he says.

"You know I'm seeing someone, right?"

"Oh pleeeaaase, you know, the more the merrier I always say." He sniffs up the line.

"We were all out the other night and she's sweet on you, honey. We all agreed, you're a hottie." I motion for him to finish up the coke left on the toilet.

He has no idea, Dina and I have been screwing around for a couple of months now. There's no way I'd tell him. No secrets with him. He lives to gossip. Dina and I both are living with lovers and he's the last one we'd want to know about us.

"Well next time you go out with Dina, count me in, we'll do some tequila," I say checking my nostrils in the mirror.

"Okay, will do lover boy. Thanks for the buzz." I'm out the door.

Brandon turned me onto a variety of mescal and tequilas one night. I've been skipping beer and wine ever since. Like they say, 'Wine is fine but liquor's quicker'.

Rounding the corner by the broiler I head towards the storeroom, stopping dead in my tracks. Dina's boyfriend is with her at the back door. Her long dark hair practically touches her butt.

"Here are your keys. They were on top of the fridge. I'll be back Monday sometime. I'll call when I leave San Diego," he says. I stand by, unnoticed, several yards away,

"Thanks for my keys." She kisses him. It bothers me. "Be sure to tell your mom and everyone in La Jolla I said 'Hi and I'm sorry I couldn't go.'"

Her boyfriend sees me over her shoulder, his bug eyes, bush eyebrows, glasses and thick mustache remind me of Groucho Marx. Dina's cool, unshaken as she greets me with bedroom eyes. Her smile, no less blinding, enticing as usual.

"Oh! Hey Nick. Stuart you remember Nick, don't you?"

"Yeah, sure. Hey, Chef, how's it going?" I nod in acknowledgement. She moves away from his embrace. I reach out to shake his hand, it's linked to a dark coat of fur covering his arm, looks like up to his shoulder.

"Hey, yeah…good to see you, Stuart." He's one of those new computer nerds.

I grab a couple of skewers of shrimp from the fridge behind me and throw them on the grill. Nothing breaks the ice better than food, I believe.

"You guys into some shrimp?" I ask.

"Suuure!" He says.

I brush them with a simple lime, cilantro and cumin marinade we use.

"La Jolla, huh? I hear it's beautiful down there." Not cheap either.

"Yeah… my mom's birthday, figured I surprise her."

I flip the shrimp. Another minute and they'll be done. Dina's watching me brush the skewer again to glaze it. I admire her glowing smile and eyes again. I know her tan lines well. They are magazine worthy of a centerfold. Hugh Heffner would hire her in a minute.

I don't know what she sees in Stuart. Must be his money or something because she lies and cheats on him. It's like Beauty and the Beast.

Suddenly I picture Gina and Patsy together, my heart drops, I still just don't get that.

I take the skewers off and wrap a foil sheet around the bottom and hand one to each of them. I'm thinking his bushy arms in the kitchen would be a nightmare even if he doesn't roll his sleeves up.

"The shrimp looks awesome, thanks," he says, as Dina pulls one up off her brochette.

"Ooh, ooh. Hot. Hot. Let it cool a bit, Stuart!" She blows on it.

"I really need to hit the road," he says. Dina turns and leans into him.

"Drive safe." She pecks him on the cheek. "Remember to call me when you leave on Monday."

"Thanks for the shrimp Nick." He darts out the back door and it swings shut. I look to Dina and she's licking her fingers.

"Sooo good, mmmm."

"So Stuey has to go home to see his Mommy?" *Wimp*, I think to myself.

"Oh, be quiet. At least he's not sleeping with someone old enough to be his mother!" Dina knows Debbie. They met a couple times over the last couple of months here at work.

I ignore her jibe. "So, are we sleeping at my place or yours? Debbie's out of town too."

"Then that's a no brainer. She has a VHS player. We could rent a video on the way to your place, she says."

"Yeah, okay. I'll need to run across the street to Tower Records before they close,"

"Oh no...you'll be in there forever."

"In and out...I promise." But I've been known to spend a couple of hours in there working on my next cassette "mix."

****

I awaken to a sharp needlelike pain in my right thigh. My eyes try to focus on my surroundings as my hand instinctively reaches down to feel my leg.

Dina begins to stir next to me. My hand finds the cause of my pain under the sheets.

I take a closer look as my eyes focus, a gold earring.

Dina stirs and mumbles, "Coffee..."

I have no idea whose jewelry it is, but it's a good thing that Debbie didn't find it.

Dina extends her arm across my chest, gently pulling me closer, with her face still in the pillow.

"Hey, is this your earring?" I ask.

"Mmmhhm huh?"

I hear something, and listen carefully. *Nah… it's nothing.* I hold the earring in front of Dina's face. "Is this your…"

"Nick…Honey, hey do you know whose car is in my parking spot?"

Debbie!

I turn to Dina and nudge her hard and whisper urgently. "Hey, hey Dina, get up, c'mon get up!"

She quickly jerks upright, topless, and begins rubbing the sleep from both eyes with her fists just as Debbie enters. As I pull up my shorts, my eyes are focused on Debbie's face, but hers are on Dina's chest.

Dina suddenly drops her hands from her eyes and pulls up the sheet to cover herself. Debbie gasps. Her eyes fill with tears. She just turns around and leaves.

Dina jumps out of bed and without a word, is dressed in seconds.

I quickly follow Debbie to the kitchen.

"Go away please. Just get away from me," she says rather calmly, to my surprise.

"Okay. Okay." As I try to think of what to say next, Dina slips past us and is out the door in a flash.

"I'm so stupid, stupid, stupid. I knew you were screwing around, I just knew it! That's Dina right…from work?" Debbie asks.

"Yeah, but it's nothing serious. It was this one time. We had drinks and well…." she looks closely in my eyes.

"You liar." She shakes her head slowly. 'You need to get out. Just leave."

"Wait, wait hold on, I'm telling you this was the only time." I lie again.

"Go. Just go. I'm not that stupid. The sad thing is, I knew it. And it wasn't just one time or girl I'm sure. I ignored the obvious. But in my house? In my bed? You make a fool of me in front of my neighbors I've known for years? Go, just go, and move in with her. I knew this was coming."

What the hell does she expect of me? She's like so much older; she had to know I might fool around by now. I figured she'd be all right with it when she's away flying all over the place.

I can't believe that she'd think there's a future with a guy twenty years younger. Who knows what she wants I mean, I thought I did. It was pretty obvious at one time, sex. For a while now I'm thinking that's what they all want. Why can't she just overlook this?

It takes no time to gather my things, my duffle bag, my suitcase, and now a few boxes. I'm placing them in my car as the door suddenly opens and my satchel comes flying out spilling some of my papers onto the pavement. My notebook spins across the asphalt and stops at my feet, as the door slams shut.

I haven't opened it in a year, haven't even seen it in months. I don't know what to make of this or how to deal with it. What I need right now is a big bong hit and to get ready for work.

I'll just get into work a bit early and wash up in the bathroom. I'll see Lionel at the photo shoot today. I'll ask if I can crash with him until I find a place. If not, I could find a cheap motel for a couple of nights, until I can work this thing out with Debbie or find a place.

****

It's 9:30 am and I'm all washed up. I've sharpened my knives, have a clean apron on and there are just a couple of top buttons left to fasten on my chef's coat. Just a quick blast and I'll be ready to roll. Lionel should be here any minute; he's always in way before Chef. I lean into a thick line on the back of the toilet and inhale just as the bathroom door opens. It must be Lionel. I stand upright and sniff up the rest with a loud snort.

"Hey Lionel, dude, I have a question for you, bro."

The stall door opens. It's the chef. The rush from the coke is quickly overwhelmed by my sudden mortification.

"What the hell are you doing?" I look as Chef eyes the rolled dollar bill in my hand and what's left of the coke on the toilet tank. His broad stature, deep voice, and authority, surprise and intimidate me.

"Oh yeah, umm…hey Chef." I slip the bill into my pants and turn towards him, blocking the toilet. His aftershave is evident.

"What are you doing Nick? You sniffing that crap?"

"No..no…nothing, ya know, just getting ready for work."

"No need. Get yourself and that crap outta here son, you're fired."

"No, hey Chef… no, really. It'll never happen again." He's not moved in the slightest.

"I know that crap goes on, Damn… but I can't turn my head when it's in my face…you gotta go." *Just like that?*

"Seriously? I promise really, never again." I plead as my heart's racing.

"And don't expect me to refer you elsewhere when you're doing that crap first thing in the morning. It's poison. That's a real issue. I suggest you get help son."

"Yes, I mean No.. it's not an issue I swear."

"It's nine o'clock in the morning. That's an issue," he says.

I have no answer for that and follow him out of the bathroom like a lost puppy towards the kitchen. It's so unfair; everyone in that place is doing it. I want to tell him that.

"You know they carried John Belushi out dead from the Chateau

Marmont up the road not long ago. What are you, stupid? It's illegal for a reason."

John Belushi OD'd. Yeah, but he was injecting it mixed with heroin. *Big difference*, I think.

"I know Chef, I know."

"And you think Richard Pryor was trying to be funny doing drugs then lighting himself up soaked in rum 151! He was killing himself."

"No Chef, it's not funny, and I don't think so." *Freebasing cocaine, I hear, is screwed up, makes you do crazy things.*

"You disappoint me, Nick. You're a good kid and you can cook. I picked you out of many others. But I can't have you doing that crap while working. I've seen people self-destruct and others always suffer for it as well. Pick up your final check on payday. Talk to me in six months if you get help and stop that crap."

"Yes, Chef. I'm sorry…thank you. Okay, will do." *I'll get my job back, it's not like I'm physically addicted, like heroin or something. I can stop this.*

I gather my things and head quickly to the door before I break, and cry. Lionel's walking in as I'm on the way out with my stuff.

"Hey Nick, good morning… Where you off to, bro?"

"Dude… Chef just busted me doing blow. I'm fired."

"What! No shit? It's nine o'clock in the morning man…what the hell?"

I'm about to choke up, but I suck it in, clinging to whatever pride I have left.

"I gotta go bro… I'll call you. Need to ask you something,"

"Sure… sure, dude. Call me soon. I'll talk to Chef," he says.

"No, please don't… he's set on this. He's old school and he's right."

Chef's words, his concerns, calling me 'son' had serious weight. Things my father would've said.

"You sure?

"Yeah, I'm sure. Sucks. Everyone in that place is doing it, and I get fired."

"It may seem like a bad thing, but hey, you never know what could happen next. The choices that will come."

I want to bang my head against the steering wheel. I don't understand how the last year just blew up in my face in just a few hours.

Will Chef screw my chances for a position in other top restaurants? Those doors won't open without his reference, and he knows the best places out here.

The moment when he walked into that stall plays with my mind and I feel like a damn fool. I hit myself in my head again just thinking about it. Seeing someone snorting coke, I'm pretty sure it's not a morning habit he's used to seeing.

A line at nine in the morning probably would have shocked me a year ago. Nights and mornings are muddled for some reason, a new norm. Well, ever since Pauly's call about Gina's accident, my life lately is such a blur. But right now, I feel it's going backwards. I'll seriously miss working these photo shoots with Chef. There's so much more I need to learn.

I push the cigarette lighter in, put the coke in my visor pocket and reach for the half of joint in the ashtray. Gonna be a long day.

****

I've seen lonely times when I could not find a friend...

~ James Taylor

I wake to somebody prodding my back. I slowly peel my cheek off a sticky lacquered wooden bar. Hazily, with double vision, I see a stripper swirl awkwardly on a chrome pole connected from stage to ceiling in front of a wall of mirrors.

174

Beer blended with the stale smokiness of the full ashtray in front of me fills my nose. There's drool on the side of my mouth, I feel it cooling on my face as it slides down past my chin. I draw my forearm across my face in slow motion, wiping it onto my sleeve.

"Okay, gentlemen, let's give a big hand for Bambi."

I hear like two people clap.

"C'mon, you're outta here. Quit drooling on the bar, man," says whoever poked me.

"Wha…whaat, huh. What the hell?" I mumble.

"C'mon, get up."

I turn as he kicks the bar stool. It's the manager of this topless-bikini bar in the mini-mall not far from where I've been staying. He was the only one here when I walked in this morning at 11, when they opened. Last night slowly comes back to me, unfolding like a mystery.

I bounced around cheap bars with a couple of tattooed shady dudes I met through Manny, the busboy with the blow. We split an eight ball of coke. The sun was up by the time we finished it. Three and a half grams, I think one or two of the dudes even smoked some at one point and called Manny again.

Then Denny's? Yeah…eggs. Right, punk rock chicks… yeah. Joints at Griffith Park? I think, dunno,..

"I said… get up man!" This guy means it. "Go home and sleep."

Home… yeah right.

I've been living with Lionel for the last several months. Debbie kicked me out last September. Tried working it out with her, we ended up having sex. But neither of us was interested in living together anymore. She was getting all New Age and spiritual, 'channeling' and crap, whatever that is. It was getting too weird for me.

Go home and sleep, the dude says. *Hah.* I'm so far from home; it's three thousand miles to New York and that's still not far enough. It seems I want to get as far away from the truth as possible. Working my second Christmas season out here helped keep me far from having to face my Mom and explain some things. My head just drops back onto my hands.

"That's it!" The guy says.

The dude pulls me up off the stool and starts pushing me towards the door.

"C'mon man, don't push, dude." Another dancer takes the stage, stirring me back to life.

"Okay, gentlemen, let's give a warm welcome to Harmony, our midwest farmer's daughter!" The DJ says.

"One more dancer, bro… now check her out." I tell him. I've learned there're no two sets of breasts alike and I've been on a quest lately to see them all. But she looks young, like, not cool young. Like she's not even legal to drink, most likely a runaway looking for the spotlight.

I guess she found it.

He pushes me through the door and I stumble into another bright sunny day in LA. What else is new? My eyes squint painfully from the sun. I reach into my car and grab my shades and leave it parked in front of the place. I need to walk this off and maybe get a bite. I start heading a couple of blocks over to Hollywood Blvd.

I'm off work, again, today. I've been working part time with several caterers lately. Some private events here and there around LA, but it's off season. Not much happening.

It's over sixth months already, but I can't speak to Chef about working the shoots with him again yet. That fact is confirmed seeing my reflection in the glass of a storefront. My hair's long, hippy long, needs a comb. My face has thinned out. I don't seem to eat much when I'm not at work. A diet of cocaine just makes you hungry, for more coke. I scratch under my chin and hear the stubble, haven't shaved in days.

Turning a corner, I look down at the smooth pink stars on Hollywood Blvd. I read the names of supposed stars and realize I don't know any of these people in this part of the Boulevard. Never even heard of them.

Some movie stars, their names make it into stone, but eventually are looked down upon as we trample them underfoot. Ironic.

My father talked about the saint's stories a lot. Hell, some of those guys lived thousands of years ago and people still talk about them, pray to them. Crazy. But there's a lot of universities, hospitals, and cities named after them out here. *San Diego, San Francisco, San Juan Capistrano, Santa Monica and San Bernardino*, a bit more than a couple of feet of sidewalk.

My Dad and Mom met at the *San Genaro Feast* in the Bronx he told me. That guy died like fifteen hundred years ago. The saints must have been quite the rock stars back in their day. They're still throwing huge parties for them, parades even.

I pass a sushi place. They've been popping up all over. I've been getting into the bento boxes and some of the sushi rolls.

I'd like to learn how to do it authentically... but getting into a Japanese or even a Chinese kitchen isn't easy. Besides, in terms of any language barrier, they choose Spanish over English every time when hiring I heard. And there're plenty of amigos to help them in the kitchen out here.

Many of the top chefs in the trendy restaurants seem to have a good Japanese assistant or sous chef in the kitchen with them. It gives them an edge by using some eastern techniques and ingredients, it keeps their dishes new and exciting.

An A-frame sign on the sidewalk up the block reads "Free Gift", and points to the street corner. Now that's a neat gimmick, I think.

Free. As I near the sign a man thrusts a pamphlet into my right hand just as another takes a step onto a milk crate, holding up a tattered book.

"In the beginning was the Word," he bellows. "The Word was with God and the Word was GOD." He speaks in a booming voice to the passersby.

I just keep walking. *Jesus Freaks.* Just like Elton John said, "… handing tickets out for God."

You see all types on this sidewalk. I take a look at the pamphlet's title. It reads, "WORD" in big letters; below the title it says,

"HOPE sees the invisible, feels the intangible and achieves the impossible" - Helen Keller.

What the hell is this psychobabble? I toss it in a wastebasket. Sometimes I feel sorry for those people, even angry at their stupidity; they're so lost. It's hard watching my mom and sister believe in that crap.

Well, it's two in the afternoon, time for breakfast and there's a burger stand not far from here that I like. It's just an open square structure with some stools surrounding a greasy griddle and a couple of guys pumping out cheeseburgers and beer.

I avoided them like the plague when I first came out. Never was into fast food and the drive thru's. But eventually after a few late nights they grew on me. The 'roach coaches' selling burritos and fish tacos outside the clubs grew on me as well. Street food. I could do this, easy. Make good money, a living anyway.

Burgers sizzle and shrink in fat on the griddle in front of me. I stand rummaging my pockets for cash. Twenty-eight bucks and change. Enough for breakfast, a couple of beers and a dime bag from the brothers at the lot on Highland and Yucca.

It's paycheck to paycheck since I've been out of Debbie's and between jobs. My college savings has been depleted for months.

Lionel was cool to let me crash when I left Debbie's. I was glad when he said I could stay, it helped a lot. We shared a lot about our lives, our childhoods. I told him everything one drunken night. All about my mom and family, how my dad died, Gina, everything.

I sip my beer. Last night's all-nighter was nothing compared to last week's. When I woke up from a nightmare in some strange girl's bed.

I've had bad dreams before, but this one, this one last week, was the real deal. I was in this realm of sleep where I thought I could wake myself, but I couldn't. I kept falling back into a surreal thick darkness. I kept trying to force myself awake again, when I'd hear the wailing and try to swim up and out of it, only to succumb back to that foggy, eerie shrieking scenario where my mind's drenched with dread. Then that damn dog appears, pursuing me, determined. It gains on me, but I don't dare turn to face it, preferring to try and hide in my darkness, so I turn and bolt. I run, swiftly, to hide in the darkest corners, only to find myself suddenly lost in some labyrinth. A maze that gets darker with despair, and more disturbing around every bend. It's past death itself, on route to some second death, much worse than the first. I try hard to escape, to find the blackest place to rest. There is no place dark enough to rest where its piercing eyes cannot find me. The more drained I feel, the closer it gains on my heels. The sheer terror of facing it, exposing myself fully to it, is overwhelming I avoid it at all costs and the chance I'll ever escape its bite seems impossible.

I finally woke up, for real, in a leaking waterbed that's half empty. I had a throbbing headache and someone half naked stirring next to me. A long brunette wig was sitting on a dresser. It shocked the hell out of me to the point I was shaking. The nappy hair on the back of the person's head gave me the chills, and a flashback to 'Monique'. I couldn't remember a thing about the night before, other than being at a strip club and the nightmare I just awoke from.

Sitting up I sank my bare feet into a soggy old shag carpet, grabbed my shirt from an armchair. Straightening my hair in the mirror I saw my mom's diamond stud was missing from my ear. Next thing I know I'm digging through the deep soaked shag carpet in this strange bedroom getting my hands and knees cold and wet. I got a closer look at the person I slept with, not the prettiest picture, one of the strippers from the night before, and sure to be a one-nighter.

She opened her eyes, her ear and cheek still mushed into the pillow, then asked me.

"What are you looking for, Nick?" She knows my name?

"I lost something. Must have dropped it somewhere. An earring." She got out of bed with the body of a smokin' dancer and pulls the earring out of her top drawer and turned to me.

"Here, you almost traded it for a half gram of coke last night," she says. I knew the guy and stopped it. It was a bad deal."

I nodded, acknowledging she's telling the truth, my sad truth. "Damn…thank you. I'm really sorry… I need to run" I remember saying. My eyes took in one last look at her body and I can see why I ended up there. I bolted out the door, not even sure if we did it or not. Yet see no reason why we didn't. I had no idea of her name and left hoping I wasn't taking AIDS with me. It's all over the news, the warning ads are scary and everywhere. People are dying. And nobody can seem to stop it. They say condoms are the answer, but I haven't carried them since Debbie.

And with that observation, I realize another sad truth— the nightmare I woke up from that day, hasn't really ended.

It's been an hour or two since I peeled my face off the bar in the strip club, I turn the key into Lionel's place and head into the kitchen to grab a beer. I drop into a chair at the table.

"Nick?" Lionel asks from around the corner.

"Yeah. Hey, good morning."

"Good morning? It's afternoon dude. All-nighter?"

"Afternoon… sorry." I hold up the Bud Tallboy. "Liquid lunch."

"A little hair of the dog, I see," he says.

"Yeah, well that was last week, she didn't bite, but she left her hair on the dresser."

"I don't wanna know. Been there…remember," he says.

"Yeah, yeah. Hey, I'm gonna have to get you the rent with next week's check. Is that okay?"

"Yeah… sure."

"Hey, I was thinking, with a few bucks I can open one of those hamburger stands you know. Those guys make a ton of cash." I look for a reaction on his face and see none. "I can come up with a new French- fry or topping, like chili burgers or something."

"Seriously. Nick, you want a burger stand?"

"Well yeah…uh sure. Or how about a food truck…ya know. I'll pull up to worksites during the day and hit outside the clubs at night. I can make kebobs or quesadilla's or something."

"So, you want to build your culinary future in a burger stand or a roach coach now, huh?"

"They make good money. Gotta pay the rent." I look at him, and then down at my beer. I want to down it so bad, but resist. He takes a seat across from me.

"Hey, listen… closely," he looks serious. 'My friend's offer in New York still stands."

I remember he mentioned something to me a few weeks ago.

"Yeah, his place and that job in mid-town?" It was a big move. I didn't give it a second thought.

"Yeah that friend, right. The apartment is furnished and he's gone; it's empty. He's working in Europe for a year at least. He just needs someone to occupy it. You'll pay a minimum, some maintenance fees."

"I don't know, man." I'm uncomfortable just thinking about getting that close to home.

"It's a high-end kitchen. The chef I told you about is top notch. I've done shoots with him, well respected in New York. I just have to call and the door will be open. You'll need to interview and then pull your weight if you get it."

I really want to guzzle that beer.

"Which I believe you can do. I've seen you work. You got this."

"You don't think my own food truck would kick-ass?" I say lightly.

"Food truck, seriously? You're shrinking out here man. Get back to New York. There's a lot of talent there. Hey your family is more important than you may think. And this place doesn't hire every day. He throws out resumes by the dozens."

"You trying to get rid of me man?"

"Look, I believe in you. Someone believed in me, gave me a chance, and I'm just paying it forward. It's a great opportunity Nick. Forget the burger stand. Stick with your dream, keep the vision. I'm not saying it won't be tough there, but I know you'll like it."

"I'll think about it…. seriously. Thanks"

"It's a good move, trust me.

****

Two weeks later I'm looking in the mirror in a restroom at LAX. I can see the top of my ears for the first time since middle school. It's a clean cut, kinda like my Dad used to have. I have a restless stomach, butterflies, nervous about this move back to New York.

And confused about what I've said and didn't say to different people back East over the years. I'll need to get my story straight. The lies have become compounded, complicated.

"Your mom must be pretty excited, huh?" Lionel's asks, waiting outside the bathroom.

"Yeah, yeah she's thrilled I'll be home in time for Easter," I say.

"You must be pretty excited too, it's been a while."

"To be honest, I'm not sure I'm ready." I look down at my new jeans and sneakers. "We haven't spoken over the last year much. My fault."

But first I'll be checking out this apartment, and meeting with the chef, ya know get my schedule and stuff." I pull out a piece of paper with all the info, checking it out closely.

"I'm glad you called him when I told you to. It's cool he hired you over the phone, that's unusual."

"Yeah, Thanks to you. He drilled me a bit, but I'm in. I'll have a probation period for six months and up for a promotion in a year."

"Like I told you, he's a strict Swiss guy with a lot of European experience, he's got a brilliant Japanese sous chef and they're creating new things, mixing traditional things up in the food world. Totally American cuisine."

His words frighten and excite me. I don't know what I'd have done without Lionel the last several months. I haven't even spoken to Chaz. I feel Lionel is what it's like to have a caring big brother.

"Hey, Lionel I really want to thank you. Really, thank you for believing in me bro," I'm about to choke up when he puts his arm around me.

"*You* just keep believing in *you,* that's the key my man, it's in you. Pick up your spa plan, be open to changes and keep on keeping on, no matter what happens." I nod in agreement, he continues.

"Life happens, it hits hard at times, but it can't keep you down, unless you let it." He looks me square in the eye. "Make right choices, like I think this one is. Quit feeding your demons and they'll die. Now, go catch that flight, hands off the stewardesses. I'll be sure to see you when I'm in the Big Apple."

I feel like I'll owe him big for this, yet he doesn't ask for a thing. He's just a generous guy. The last thing I want to do is screw this up.

Five and a half hours later my eyes open to the sun rising over the Atlantic Ocean from my window seat. We roll to a stop at Kennedy. Losing the three hours overnight from Pacific Time is what gives these 'red-eye' flights their appropriate name.

There's Teddy. He's broader, like he's been lifting, a cop in the South Bronx now. His firm handshake and a slap on the back greet me at the baggage carousel.

"Hey Teddy. Thanks for picking me up." It's good to see a real childhood friend again.

"Don't mention it man. So good to see you," he says with a huge grin.

Funny how the military wouldn't take him, but the cops in New York did; they must be really shorthanded. He's in a rough neighborhood, just the way he likes it he said. His rusty hair has a neat cut, a new ruddy mustache and mirror sunglasses over his high rosy cheekbones, scream plainclothes Irish cop to any criminal who's on the lookout for that. He's more reserved, respectful, a gentleman.

I just hope he doesn't peek in my bag because I smuggled some California bud in. And I don't need a lecture on it now. I don't know what he'd do as a cop, but he always hated weed.

"Whoa, heyyy, look at you man, looking sharp. How's New York treating you?

"New York? They're calling it the Rotten Apple." He takes off his shades revealing his steel blue eyes and chiseled face. "Times Square is all drugs, pimps, runaways, and porn theatres. The mayor sucks, and we get to protect the sleaziest people and tourists you've ever seen."

"So, it's not much different from when I left."

He gives a short, grim laugh. "No … except for more crack heads, growing heroin epidemic. Oh, and whatever this 'AIDS' is, it's filling the hospitals."

"I know, LA too. Some scary stuff."

"Where's this studio apartment you're subletting anyway?"

I pull out the address Lionel gave me and open it.

"439 West 47th street. I have to get the key from the neighbor in apartment 4C."

Another laugh, this one even shorter. "Well I hope your neighbor with the key is nicer than the neighborhood. Because you're smack in the middle of it all man. That's Hell's Kitchen buddy. Welcome home…"

Chapter Twelve

The Living Years

"And if you don't give up, and don't give in,
You may just be O.K…"

~ Mike and the Mechanics

THE RISING SUN LIGHTS THE graveyard as I near it, just a few miles from my mom's in the suburbs. Headstones line the landscape in neat rows and much of the surrounding trees look dead, void of leaves, some show signs of buds, Spring, emerging. Mini purple tulip-like flowers, poke through the dead leaves. I used to know their name. There's freshness in the air. Humidity, frozen all winter, has thawed. Green grass easily overcomes last season's dead withered blades.

Actually, the place seems full of life at this time in the morning. Already seen squirrels, rabbits and deer. Wild turkeys rustle through the leaves on the edge of the woods. Taking the early bus up was a good idea. Been a long time, I needed to come.

Tomorrow's Easter Sunday and a strong desire to visit here before I settle at my mom's for the weekend overwhelmed me.

It's harder than I thought, stepping up to Gina's stone. She's right beside the tall twin pines, similar to the ones in our yard. Right where my mom said she would be.

A fresh palm frond cross is staked into the ground centered in front of it. It's well tended to with edging and mulch. A bouquet of bright cut flowers stands upright in a green metal holder. Sprouting plants push through the soil.

Those tiny tulips flowered here as well…a white variety. Her name's engraved in rosy colored granite, strategically placed below a sculpted angel with open wings.

Just the thought of her parents kneeling in the dirt, tending to her grave crushes me. The pressure pierces my chest and an overwhelming sense of grief and guilt invades me.

189

The last time I went to mass with Gina was Palm Sunday. Afterwards we came here with my family said a prayer, and placed a palm cross at my dad's stone.

Raising my nose to the sky, I take a couple of deep breaths to prevent tears. The morning sun is direct, strong, rising over the trees, and warming my shoulders. I pull a single cellophane wrapped red rose from my travel bag and gently place it on her head stone. I fight for better thoughts.

Closing my eyes, I'm comforted by a memory I see, my first Valentine's Day card to Gina. Red construction paper, a doily, Elmer's glue, some scissors and I had a card that folded open to a big heart. I felt strongly about personally making hers. All the other kids got the generic, assorted, store-bought ones. I was too young for corny. But I'll never forget what I wrote, the old standby with a slight change.

Roses are red; violets are blue,
Sugar is sweet, and I think you're COOL!

'Cool' was the new word in my vocabulary and I started using it a lot.

I remember we were in awe and in wonder of everything; bugs, birds, trees, streams, frogs, rain, and storms. Every moment with Gina, was fun. Even when things went wrong we'd laugh and end up learning something.

She was true, trustworthy, and never changed from that 'cool' childhood friend I had since I was six. Never tainted by peers or poor choices. And in the twelve out of eighteen years of knowing each other I recall how we were inseparable.

Hard to believe I was ever that young, or innocent. Everything seemed awesome to me back then. Every moment, everything, was full of life. Like this place this morning, I felt part of something much bigger then. Dreams were easily born in the still moments.

What could possibly make sense of this? Who can explain her dying so young?

When I think of the last day I saw her and how I upset her about moving west, I choke up. I can clearly see her running towards her house, crying. But I realize now my disregard for her personal choice, her pregnancy, our situation, must have really disturbed her about me.

My thoughts aren't helping as the guilt is compounding. The accident must have been horrific for her. An oncoming car, Patsy passed out driving, I can hear her screaming in my head, like when she was assaulted by Ace at the grad party. Except this time, I can do nothing.

The dark void I feel inside me expands. Overwhelming any happy memory as I realize that part of me, Gina's love, is gone and can never be filled again. A black hole that only despair seems to fill now but is never satisfied.

Looking around at hundreds of headstones, I turn back to Gina's. I gaze at her name, and notice the dash between the year she was born and when she died. 1963 - 1981. I glance around again with a realization, everyone's life, is in that small dash. One short dash that's all you get.

The dream we started together, I realize, may have died with her. It's been out of my focus now, far from the hope we once had together. If I could only turn back time... choices.

I pull a joint out of my top pocket, light up and take a big hit, cos' my next stop here won't be any easier. Smoking weed this time in the morning pretty much sets the rhythm for the day. It isn't like eating my Wheaties. I blow through more pot when I start early, cos' I'll continue smoking throughout the day. Which reminds me, I need to get some and I don't want to call Pauly or my friends to see where.

Being tight with my buddies back in grade school was easy, natural, and true. And it's something about those days, those years that connected a pure part of us. Way before the sway from older 'cool' kids.

I guess we were looking to grow up faster at some point because we were all underage when we got into to beer and pot. It became all we'd do and talk about, our secret. And with it came lies, mischief, and trouble. Honesty with our parents was gone by thirteen.

I suddenly realize what's connected us since grade school for years may be just that. The drinking, smoking, and drugs; our secret life and lies.

Man, the last thing I need with this new job, is to hook up with them again. I heard things haven't changed much around here, and I don't need any more secrets. I got more than my share in LA.

I'm in a familiar row of gravestones. I remember seeing them every Sunday, in every season since I was a kid. My mom had us all come to the cemetery, pay respects and tend to my Dad's gravesite. We sometimes clean his headstone, *Nicholas Vincent Anselmo.*

My mom's here a lot I can tell. A palm cross is staked between potted Easter Lilies. A small statue of Saint Joseph sits on the stones base, which I'm pretty sure my sister Trisha put there. The bronze New York firefighter's marker hasn't moved from where his Fire Chief placed it years ago. I remember hundreds of firemen here, so many; they needed cops to control the traffic around town. As much as I thought I would grow to be like him… I'm so not.

I miss his strong warm hand on my shoulder that would squeeze me close every so often. His voice reassuring, his aftershave, a sense of security. Patience when I made mistakes. His encouragement. Always celebrating my smallest successes while never doubting the larger ones to come.

These thoughts strike a chord in me. When did I go against

everything my father shared and stood for? Was there a moment where I said, I got this? I know better, it's my way.

Because the more I try standing on my own, the more I'm sinking down. I lose all the fuzzy feelings I just had remembering my dad in an instant.

The day he died floods back into my mind and triggers more than just a need for a buzz. More like something to numb me, to help me deal with this when these thoughts happen, but it's too late, there's no escape. Here we go again, like a replay in my mind.

That day in my room when I threw the ball, I threw the ball... *why'd I have to throw the ball??* The screeching tires, air horn, Joey's screams, Trisha's wailing; my mom in the street clutching my dad's bloodied head in her lap.

But's it's always the finality of him being lowered into the grave right here below my feet, that really hits me. The moment people placed flowers on his casket; my mom trying to be strong as Trisha and Joey cling to her dress.

I feel weak, and drop onto my knees in front of his headstone. My insides scream so much that I want to let it out, cry out loud. I open my mouth but I'm breathless, nothing sounds, tears fall as I wheeze to catch my breath.

A passing sun shower sends a short-lived downpour through the graveyard and dampens me. But the sun's rays soon turn it into steam that rises evaporating all around me. I take notice of the dash between the dates on his headstone and think again of the shortness of life. Nobody gets out alive. Sniffling, I suck up my tears and stuff them back inside. I need to get going.

My mom's probably already cooking for tomorrow and I'm here to help her out today. The many little fibs I've told her have grown over the years to the point that I'm not even sure what my story is anymore. This is not an easy morning and isn't going to be an easy Easter.

I kind of wish I had to work.

****

The aroma of my mom's Easter soup fills my nose as I enter the kitchen and kiss her on the cheek. It's been a while since I've smelled it. Well over a year since my graduation. She's rolling out dough on the kitchen counter, but she drops the rolling pin, turns, and hugs me. Tight. Really tight and for a long time.

"Happy Easter, honey. Help yourself to coffee and biscotti or I can make eggs. We'll get started whenever you're ready." I hear her sniffle as she turns, and I think she may be crying. She gets right back into rolling out the dough.

The familiar smells of the holiday bring my childhood front and center in my mind and melt any fear of discussion about LA that might pop up. The aroma of baking Easter breads stirs my appetite; I open the oven to see what's cooking.

"The Easter Vigil starts at ten o'clock tonight. I hope you brought something nice to wear," Mom says.

Damn, that's like two or three hours long. I figured we'd be going to mass, but the vigil?

"Oh, we're going to the vigil tonight? Not mass tomorrow?" Easter Sunday is just about an hour, usually.

"Yes, it's very nice. You really used to like it…remember? And we've been going to it for the last couple years."

"Sure, okay…yeah I have something to wear." It's no suit and tie that's for sure.

We all went to the vigil when my dad was alive. It was cool, as a kid. They gave everyone an unlit candle and shut the lights. The whole church would be completely dark. Like the darkness of the world. Then someone with one lit candle from outside represents the "light" of the world, Jesus. One by one, the light of the one candle lights another, each lighting their neighbor's until and the whole place becomes lit in a warm glow. But the year after my dad died, it took forever for that mass to end.

"Nicky, please fill a pot of water to boil the pasta for the macaroni pie and make sure you drop plenty of salt in it."

"Sure mom…so where we at with all the cooking?" There's a lot of cooking ahead. That… I know, I wash up briskly at the kitchen sink.

"Well let's see… you're boiling the pasta. We'll need to break a lot of eggs for that, the 'pizzagaina' and the ricotta cheesecake, so, about three flats. Oh, and boil two dozen, some for the sweet bread and the rest for Trisha and Kelly to color. Save some eggs to drop into the soup tomorrow, about six."

"Okay, got it. What else?"

"Cut up all the cold cuts and cheese ends for the pizzagaina too. But first dice up the pancetta and get it cooked off for the pork bread, and save the grease, please."

The macaroni pie is just various pastas, eggs mixed with cream or half and half, Romano cheese, and salt and pepper.

If you don't get enough salt into the pasta water during the boiling process it could come out bland and you end up adding salt to the surface only, which makes it vary. It's a simple dish with a neutral flavor, so it can take on whatever you add to it.

I've had it warm with butter and Parmesan, sweet with raisins and honey even. But its usually served room temperature drizzled with olive oil, grated cheese and ground black pepper.

But my favorite is slightly warm with white truffle oil, grated Locatelli cheese and black pepper. This kitchen never sees fresh truffles, but I played with them out west.

195

My mom tends to lean towards the southern, Neapolitan dishes. But macaroni pie is what we'll eat tonight, because the day before Easter is considered a fast day– eat in moderation, no meat and be mindful of the 'Holy-Day' as mom would put it.

I look for the pancetta and deli-ends in the fridge. It's full with stuff for the holiday and I'm sure the fridge in the garage is full too. My mom will ask for the cold-cut ends and the deli guy will just give them to her for free; they all know her.

I break off a piece of provolone and then slice off a small chunk of capicollo and toss it in my mouth.

"Nicky…remember today's a fast day."

Right… I can't eat meat today. *Damn.* I sure don't miss my religion. I can't remember the last time I even had some good capicollo; there're few delis in LA, and they're Jewish. No ham.

"Oh geez…okay Mom." I toss another piece in my mouth as my appetite revs up. I'm getting the munchies. Okay no meat, more cheese.

In a few short hours, we're looking at fresh baked breads, desserts, and cream puff pastry ready to fill.

Uncle Lou walks in carrying packages with my brother, Joey. Haven't seen either since I left, a couple of years ago. Joey's my height. His hair is longer than mine is now and he looks like Chachi on Happy Days, dark hair, matching eyes, and wearing a sleeveless white t-shirt. I reach out to help with the packages.

"Hey, Guiseppi! Back from the Bronx already?"

They have goods from Arthur Avenue. I'm sure it's fresh mozzarella, olives, antipasto things, and a fresh leg of lamb Uncle Lou gets every year from his friend Sal the butcher.

"So, look at you, Hollywood." Uncle Lou eyes me. "Nice of you to visit."

I feel a bit of a chill in the air from them. *Nice of you to visit?*

"Hey Uncle Lou. Yeah, yeah, great to see you."

"Wassup Nick?" Joey greets me. "I heard you got back last week," he says sternly.

Now I get it.

"Yeah, hey. I'm sorry Joey, got tied up with work and my new place." I say.

"Mom called LA and your friend said you left for New York last week. She was hoping to pick you up you know."

"I didn't want to bother her. I had a real late flight and Teddy picked me up. But I told her I'd be here today. Hey… senior this year, right?"

"Yeah, senior year. A few teachers and friends keep asking about you. They think you disappeared. I didn't know what to tell them, you never call."

"Well we could catch up now." I say

I get nudged from Uncle Lou.

"Hey you… Banana," he says.

I don't know what it is with food nicknames and Italians but to be called some type of fruit or vegetable is usually an endearing term. Unless it's "eggplant" and you're black or "meatball" and you're fat. But to keep respect within the family, food names are better than real insulting crude ones. I mean we still respect food and I've heard everything from basil brain to pineapple.

"Yeah, Unc, what's up?" I answer, confirming I'm a banana.

"Come on, come check out this lamb leg I picked up and help bring in the stuff from my car."

"Yeah sure…" I say.

He turns to my brother.

"Joey, bring up the folding chairs and the card table from the basement for tomorrow."

"Yeah sure, Unc, No problem."

I follow Uncle Lou to his black Buick in the driveway. His trunk is filled with stuff. He looks directly at me, seriously.

"You know kid, nobody loves you when you have dog shit on your shoe."

"Wha…what?" I laugh a bit baffled.

"You need to watch your step. Ya know…with who and where you walk because eventually you start to smell and nobody, except the rotten ones, will stand your smell anymore."

"Yeah…I hear you Uncle Lou." I think, okay let's move on past this.

"I'm not sure you do. I don't know what you got into out there but in order for it to be more important than your family that loves you, it must have some serious pull."

Oh, man here it is. I guess I have it coming.

"And I have a feeling it's not just the T and A out there so if you're doing any of that crap that's going around… CUT IT OUT! Or I'll kill you, before you can rob yourself of your own life or ruin your mom's."

Uncle Lou's no dummy. He's been everywhere, he knows what's going around on the street. And the 80's in New York, is no better than the 70's.

"You know people are killing each other for that crack crap. And your mom is worried. She doesn't know what's up with you, and she sees that stuff even on the local news."

He looks intensely into my eyes; I think he's looking to see if I'm high. I suddenly wish I wasn't here because I could really use another buzz. I never would have expected this from Uncle Lou. I'm pretty sure he knew I smoked weed. He moves his eyes away from mine and seems frustrated.

"Ya know, your mom doesn't understand a selfish attitude or

rejection from a family member. She has never experienced it. It was unheard of before you in our family.

She would never expect that from her son, who she raised and loves might I remind you. She didn't come from that. We didn't come from that, your father didn't come from that, and you didn't either."

"It hasn't been easy, Uncle Lou. Been through some crap out there. But I'm not smoking crack. Believe me, I promise."

"Well get over whatever it is. Life isn't easy; it's not supposed to be. But it's a lot better if you quit feeding it poor choices." My head hung, focused on the pavement beneath my feet.

"Don't think you're above people because you're not the guy in the gutter. If you don't stop focusing on who's below you to feel better, you'll end up there. Start looking up or you'll never see the opportunities, the big picture."

Why is he saying this?

"Believe me, I'm not feeling too big of myself lately."

"Yeah… but you were a bit cocky when you took off a couple of years ago, ya know."

I never heard him pissed at me; he always would goof with me. I guess I never gave him reason to be mad before.

"What are you hiding from kid? You owe someone money or sumptin"? You never came to pay your respects to Gina and her family. I'd quit before working for a boss who wouldn't allow a couple of days for that."

"No… no, Uncle Lou. Things are just much different than I planned, not what I expected."

"It's life, Nick. It just means there's a better plan. Don't exchange the struggle it takes just to walk in this world for some safe place in a little box, doing stupid drugs. That's not living." He nudges my shoulder good. "Look at me…" I lift my eyes to meet his.

"No cow chooses to be veal, ya know? We have a choice. You wanna be a veal chop? Huh, do ya? "

Again, with the food, but I get it. Now I remember why I didn't want to come home.

"I hear you, Uncle Lou, but I'm not partying."

"That's good, so then don't let past regrets keep you from your dreams; admit them and move on. Drop the guilt trip. We all make mistakes… believe me…I've made more than a few. Now I want you to help me prepare this lamb leg tomorrow. I was thinking keep it simple with some rosemary and garlic. What do you think?"

"Yeah, yeah sure Uncle, sounds good." I'm happy to change the subject and I know just what to do with the lamb.

"Ya know kid, everyone thought Jesus was dead, but He got up that's what this is about ya know. We're all very excited you're home, safe, another big reason to celebrate."

He places his arm around me and squeezes my shoulders, kind of like my dad used to. He hands me the lamb tied up in brown deli paper. It's fifteen pounds at least. I tuck it under my arm and imagine preparing it, roasted simply, inserted with garlic cloves, rosemary, a bit of fresh lemon juice, kosher salt, and black pepper. I bet brushing it with some Worcestershire and oyster sauce would work well to add a nice rich flavor and color.

I'm not sure where my head is at after LA. These older chefs in Manhattan know so much about food it blows my mind. It's a strict kitchen. When they need to fill a position they only ask around within the kitchen, and if you refer someone, they better be good or it's a serious reflection on you. I'm beginning to believe it's who you know. And I'm glad I know Lionel.

The chef runs this kitchen like a Swiss watch. Lionel must have stuck his neck out for me, because this is a very reputable kitchen, highly respected in New York for years. The regulars are powerful people. Moguls, publishers and politicians.

But I'm not sure I'm feeling it right now. Not sure if I'm coming or going. There's so much more to learn. Don't know if I can stick this out, or if I want to. It's not the party kitchen I'm used to. It's like military school. And I never really liked school.

Chapter Thirteen

Dream On

"You know it's true… All the things you do, come back to you"

~ Aerosmith

IT'S A COLD APARTMENT, a five-story walk-up building on the West Side. It's all open with red brick walls and a TV hanging by a thick chain wrapped around it from the ceiling. The bed is a queen mattress on a loft that I have to climb up to, through a square hole.

Under the loft are two armchairs and a coffee table that face the TV. A cheap couch sits under a huge old double-hung window that overlooks the street and a small parking lot on the other side. On the far side of the studio is the kitchen and bath separated by a partition standing half way to the high ceiling. The shower is a tin metal cylinder with a plastic opaque curved door you slide open to enter. It looks like a contraption I saw in a weird Woody Allen movie. Next to that is a toilet, an original I guess, because it's like a hundred years old with dark stains around the hole that aren't removable.

The ceiling must be twelve feet high or more and all the heat accumulates up there. The open kitchen has a peninsula counter jutting out with two bar stools for a kitchen table. An old stove, rounded fridge and two-bay sink all are old and basic.

The four locks on the door tell me something about the area outside. There's a steel bar that swings out and leans up against the door. I never saw anything like it before. But I'm sure it'll slow down anyone trying to kick it in.

The resident cockroaches are in the kitchen and bath, and I'm sure their descendants go back several generations in this building. I haven't seen evidence of rodents, but there're plenty on the streets and in the trash at night. I've seen my share of roaches in commercial kitchens over the years. As soon as you get rid of them, others arrive tucked in somewhere in the next delivery.

This place is nothing like Debbie's tidy townhouse near Holly-wood Hills. And it's very different from Lionel's place by Melrose in West Hollywood. But it's mine and I don't miss roommates, or LA for that matter.

New York feels better, I think I missed the seasons. And people are just being themselves— no acting, however crude that may be at times. I can't say all's well though. I may be back East and closer to home in the 'burbs' but I still feel distant, far from my family. Easter was an eye opener and it's a hard fact to face. Even Trisha kept her distance and I really can't tell if it's her condition or not anymore. Mom said she's improved with the help she's getting. Maybe it's me keeping my distance from her, so she can't get all weird with me.

My tainted new surroundings in Hell's Kitchen actually aren't that bad during the day. In fact, I like it a lot. It's New York, the real deal. The West Side Story of the 80s, just nix the romance before sex and add more graffiti and hard drugs.

Irish bars are everywhere and they have the cheapest beer and shots. In between the traditional folk songs there's U2 and great rock and roll on the jukeboxes. I judge places by their jukebox, I sometimes take a half hour picking a playlist of songs before settling down at the bar.

So many people blend in odd ways around here. You don't know who's who and from where, but the tunes weave a common thread through us all. Runaways, dealers, pimps, thieves, actors, and blue-collar workers cross each other's paths here. All seem to trade places at times. Actors prostitute themselves, runaways be-come thieves, and drug dealers trade drugs for sex. Pimps are father figures, slave masters, and businessmen. And the blue-collar worker walks the thin line that could flip him to his wild side.

During the day, *The Blarney Stone* piles fresh-sliced corned beef and brisket high on rye from steam tables for a few bucks. That with

206

a cold beer and I fit right in with the union guys building the Jacob Javits Center over on 11th Ave. These guys are in the bars morning, noon, and at five. But the nights… the nights are another story.

There're gangs around, well, one in particular, it's organized. *The Westies* they run Hell's Kitchen. And Quinn, Patsy's brother, knows them well. And the less I know about them the better. But Quinn, he has some bad ambitions. Teddy tells me he still lives where he did when we were in high school. Still doing business with pills and pot. Not what I wanted to hear, a little too close for comfort, and it's already crossed my mind to visit him.

There're eyes on the street watching everything. And in an instant, a gang can form, mainly to protect its own interests in the neighborhood. And if there's money to be made or taken they'll help themselves, easiest targets first. Usually a tourist, an old lady, or a kid from Jersey looking for something he shouldn't. Anyone who's not a regular on the block, not a buyer, is a suspect, or potential victim.

It is what it is.

I keep one eye practicing peripheral vision and the other over my shoulder. Any gold or jewelry should be kept out of sight and I carry a box cutter at all times. It's important to stay alert and sharp. Too much to drink you're sure to become a victim— rolling drunks is a nighttime activity for teens around here.

There're times I wish someone would start with me just to get my frustration out. But if it were a bunch of the young kids, the 'wolf packs' that pop up, I'd be screwed. It's never one on one. They usually target businessmen or tourists. Any time of day, a swarm of six or more, 9 to 12-year-olds descend upon people and strip them clean of watches, wallets, cash, and jewelry. Anything they can hide quickly and run with. They break- up, then meet later and split the goods. They won't get much from me. Don't have it.

One reason they would avoid me is that I'm young, Italian look-ing, and there's a chance they think I'm a cop. Confident Italian and Irish guys in plainclothes can very well be cops, more so if they have a mustache. Serpico-types, undercover, you never know. Others could be on the *Westies* payroll.

I like my place, this location. My job is just across town from Park Ave and up a few blocks or so. No need to take a train. But the best part of Hell's Kitchen is Ninth Avenue. It's lined up with the largest variety of ethnic foods and markets.

Up and down the Avenue are small family run shops with foods from around the world, each competing with fresh products and prices for your business. A bazaar of spices, grains, oils, vegetables, and fruits; there're cheese shops, poultry, butchers, and fishmongers. Much of it, I still have no idea what to do with. Which excites me, cos' I'll never stop learning. Little old immigrant ladies know exactly what to do with the odd ingredients found there. Many don't speak a bit of English, are illiterate, and can't read a recipe. Untapped wis-dom and talent going back for generations; something I learned to appreciate from my own grandmothers.

But I'll spend time asking whoever can speak some English what their making. Whether Asian, Greek, Dominican, Bulgarian, Rus-sian, wherever they're from, I'm interested in the ingredients they're buying, and what they're preparing. Thanks to New York and Ninth Ave., I don't have to travel far to learn authentic world cuisine.

A few places have live rabbits, chickens, squab, quail, and pheas-ant. Pick one out and they'll do the dirty work, nothing fresher than that.

I like this new job, it's tough like Lionel said. Real serious it seems. There's no getting to work late with this chef, without hearing about it. No beards, long hair, dirty shoes, or dirty fingernails. He has his manicured. An unwritten rule is to get to work a half hour early, sit with the cooks and have a bite to eat, before starting work.

The sun beats down mercilessly between the skyscrapers as I head east of 5th Ave, where the beautiful people live. The same Sabrett hot dog I could buy one block earlier suddenly jumps fifty cents. Doormen, chauffer's, top restaurants and fountains appear. Fifth Ave is what they use to divide the classes it seems. Maybe I'll have a place here one day. But for now, it's only where I work. Where those of us who serve, find work serving.

Unlike 'new' money in LA the money here goes back so many generations that some can't care for themselves anymore. They never had to. They're quite dependent on others for the basics, like cooking a meal, opening a door, walking their dog or raising their kids. Here there are those who serve and those who are being served.

It's extremely warm for late spring, so I make a beeline through horns and traffic towards a shaved ice vendor. I have a little time to kill anyway. The exhaust and bustle of the street suddenly seem distant, as I catch a whiff of fragrance from the woman several steps ahead of me. Her slender stature in oversized faded jeans and jacket as seen from behind intrigue me. She's no slave to fashion like everyone else here. She's handing the vendor money. Her curled chestnut hair shines and falls below her shoulders. As it flows in the breeze it leads my mind to envision one of 'Charlie's Angels', Jaclyn Smith. I'm anxious to see if she looks like her. The countless crowd of people flurrying become blurred as my eyes focus on her.

That is until some scrawny, ragged, grimy guy appears out of the multitude, in a torn green army coat, clearly not into hygiene. He stands out from the crowd and slowly approaches the woman that my eyes are on, with a sick, deviant smile. It's concerning. I hear him address the vendor in a low, smoky, creepy tone while his piercing eyes send a perverse glare toward her.

"She's hot, isn't she? Yeeaaahh, I've been trailing her. Go ahead man, go ahead tell her," he says to the vendor as he's leering at her. "Tell her sheee's... foxy."

The vendor is silent, sticking to business as he hands her a cherry red ice.

"She's the sugah, right?" the strange guy says. "Gorgeous, sweet mmmm-mmmm, my goodness lovely," he continues.

I catch a glimpse as the woman turns her head to one side. My curiosity's suddenly satisfied by her profile. Man, she is beautiful. And she's not flaunting it at all; in fact, she's dressed down, baggy, but it can't hide the radiance that shines through her smooth bronze complexion. She's far from Jaclyn Smith, in my eyes, she's prettier.

She turns away from the crazy man in an attempt to leave quickly, and steps full body, square into me, spilling red ice onto my shirt. She immediately starts brushing it off my chest, instinctively. Her head below my nose, her fragrance fills it, I breathe in deeply.

"Oh my... oh no, I'm sorry, I'm so sorry," sincerely, in a soft voice as she focuses on leaving me spotless. I could care less, my eyes just want to meet with hers.

"Hey, please, just forget about it. It's fine, really." The ice brushes right off, no worries. But she eludes eye contact. I like her. Even if I have no idea what's under the baggy clothes she's wearing. It's like the first time in years it wasn't cleavage or a nice ass that got my attention.

"Excuse me, but I really need to leave... I'm very sorry," she says, quickly looking over her shoulder. The man leering at her seems to be no longer an annoyance.

"Sure. Hey, it's no problem, really. Are you gonna be okay?" I ask, still hoping to get in her line of sight as she steps away.

"Yes, yes thank you. I just need to go." Still refusing me a look into her eyes. Disappointed, I turn to the vendor.

"I'll take a lemon ice." He hesitates. "Please… sir… lemon ice?" The vendor points behind me, I turn around and see that crazy guy grab the young lady's elbow; her ice hits the cement in a red slushy splat that spreads across the sidewalk. He creepily starts stroking her hair, holding her one arm tightly. He looks down at the ice, which is quickly melting into syrupy red liquid.

"Uh oh. Oh, boy, I'm sorry sugah, lemme getcha anutha." He pulls his pockets inside out.

"Oh no, all out. Hey ya got some cash?" He says to her.

"It's okay. That's fine, sir, really I'm fine. Please… just leave me be!"

He turns back toward the vendor still holding her. My minds racing about how I can help.

"Hey…Hey, my man…let me get an ice for my suggah pie, huh?" He says to the vendor as he tightens his grip and starts pulling her back towards the stand. I'm about to say something when her face turns to me and her eyes plead directly into mine, she's frightened as hell. Her soulful, large ebony eyes earnestly cry for help. I turn full body and step towards them.

"Don't you worry my hunny bunch. We getchu anutha ice," the nut says to her.

People just keep passing, ignoring the clearly troubled situation and scene. I take another step towards them.

"Hey guy, get lost man. Listen to the lady, leave her alone," I say with weight.

He turns his focus to me. His face is gritty, wrinkled, and dark with layers of dirt, as if dried by some desert sun. His hair drops to his neck in a straggly, grey, rusty nest. He's wearing dark fingerless knit gloves, and a green hooded sweat jacket under his army coat. Ragged red cloth sneakers are half laced below tan corduroys with assorted stains. An eerie grin reveals jagged, tarnished teeth that seem more animal than human. His demeanor suddenly becomes both agitated and energetic towards me.

"Oh boy, oh boy, look at you, look at you. You talkin' to me?" His feet seem jumpy as he flails his one free hand at me. "Yeah, yeah, you are talking to me, good…yeah okay, okay good." I stand upright and straighten my shoulders.

"Oh… sure, I see, you want her too, do ya? Yeeeaaahhh, you like her, don't you? Well she's MY woman, you hear me, mine!" The man pulls her closer, and continues to awkwardly stroke her hair. I feel a nervous vibe running up the back of my neck as if my hair may stand as I take another step.

"I said GET LOST man…let her go!" this guy's nuts.

"Man o' man…o' man, o' man. You wiggin' kid? You wanna be a hero, huh? Shurre, yeah. I gotcha. You wanna fight for her. Okay, okay Slick, I like a rumble."

He slowly draws a large Bowie knife out of his sagging pants. Game changer. His grasp on the girl hasn't lessened one bit as he carefully approaches me. I step back, and see the young woman is visibly trembling.

"Hey… look man. Just let her go. Please… just back off," I say. Never saw a hunting knife nearly that big. The guy keeps coming, focused on me like he's about to devour prey. The girl is no longer trembling; she's petrified, frozen, sniffling, and sobbing in the man's grip.

"You like her, don't cha? Yeeeaahh, you want your way with her… right?? Well I seen her first, but okay, I'll fight cha for her."

He lunges at me with the knife, forcing me to back off. He aggressively thrusts again, stepping back into my space, the woman's arm still gripped in his hand. He's so close that I quickly clutch his arm with the knife firmly, immediately he passes the knife to his other hand and stands behind the woman bringing the blade, longer than her head, up to her ear. His arm squeezes her neck in a headlock.

His other hand grips my wrist twisting it painfully, bringing me to my knees before he lets go with a shove. My heart pushes adrenaline throughout my body— as my mind convicts me of making things worse. The woman's eyes are closed tight as her lips move prayerfully. I'm stunned by his quick reflex and strength. I jump up in defense as he comes at me again. *What the hell did I get into?* Every person passing avoids us, refusing to take notice by moving to the other side of the street to pass. The young woman is stiff with panic. In an instant, he could cut her, maybe kill her if I make a wrong move. I take a deep breath, afraid to act. *Think!*

I slowly step towards them, focused on him patting my side. Warning him that I have a gun. His sick smile just gets wider.

"You really need to let her go and leave, cuz I will use this." I tap my waist again firmly. The lady's face is in total distress; her eyes look to the sky as tears stream her cheeks. I can't just back off and do nothing. I stand my ground firmly, hoping, I'm doing the right thing. In that instant, a bright reflection from something comes over my shoulder from behind and levels with the crazy man's face in a bright ray of light. The guy is blinded, suddenly stupefied. He winces as the reflection dances across his face and tries to shade his eyes with his hand. I carefully take another step towards them.

"I said leave, now! You're pissing me off." I hold my hand to my side, ready to pull the gun. The woman skirmishes as he loses focus and he lets her go, pushing her hard to the side. Stumbling, she struggles to keep her balance I reach out to and she quickly takes my hand, steadying her footing before stepping behind me and flush up against my back. The lunatic paces backwards, slowly, keeping one eye on me as he's blocking the light with his hand. He slips the Bowie knife back into his pants.

"Damn! He says. "I see you. I see you there, man. I'm going. Yeah, I'm going, but I'm not done, you'll see." His long boney finger shaking as he points at me through his fingerless glove.

"I'm the monkey. I'm the monkey man, and I never sleep," he then says.

His stare is brittle, sending bad vibes up my spine. He lowers his head below his shoulders and gives one last crazy glare towards me that chills me to the bone. He slowly turns his head, flipping his hood over it, then quickly twists full body, and vanishes around the corner.

The frightened look on the woman's face disturbs me it just doesn't belong. Her beautiful eyes are glossed with tears, as she looks up to mine suddenly hugging me tight, trembling. I smooth her back, tapping it gently in hopes to comfort her. Within a couple of minutes, her shaking subsides and she takes a step back, holding my hand, smothering it with both of hers.

"Ohhh...oh, I'm sorry." she says, trying to brush tears from my shirt. "Oh God. Thank you, thank you sooo much." She returns to holding my hand, tight.

"Sorry? Hey, hey, no apologies. It's over... okay. Your gonna be fine." I reassure her.

"Oh my, I'm still shaking," she says as her eyes turn from mine moving back into my chest. The pleasant fragrance of her hair fills my nose.

"It's okay, please, don't worry, he's gone." I have goose bumps, again, but this time it's from déjà vu. Like I've met this girl before, I know her.

"I was so afraid you were going to shoot," she says.

I lift my shirt to expose my waist. "Shoot what? I have nothing to shoot." I say.

Her face is vibrant, radiant like I haven't seen since Gina. Her skin is flawless, smooth. I can't figure out what nationality she is. Maybe Indian, Pakistani or Moroccan.

"Really, I just don't know how to thank you."

Before I can say anything, she leans in and starts hugging me tight, again. I'm startled by her outward affection. She can't be from around here. I mean, it's New York; people just don't hug strangers.

"You did, you thanked me already. Hey I'm sorry, but I need to get to work." I look at my watch, and then clear my throat, "busy night ahead" I say.

This whole ordeal quickly ate up my few minutes to spare. She slowly releases me, squeezing my hand before fully letting go.

"Oh, yes…of course. I'm sorry," she says.

"Hey, you just stay safe, relax, it's over."

"Yes. Yes, I will thank you so much."

I can't stay another minute and risk being late. I'll never see her again. And I can't even imagine anyone else out there like her. She seems sweet on me but she's way out of my league I believe; some rich chick in disguise, maybe? I turn to the vendor as I bolt across the street.

"Give her another ice my man." He nods towards me.

She leaves in the opposite direction. Before I get lost in the crowd. I turn to see her and she's looking right at me from a distance. She smiles brightly, as our eyes meet again for a moment. And then she's gone. I'm glad I was able to help, but I wish I never saw her face.

After a seriously rough night at work in the kitchen, I walk onto the sidewalk sporting my new burns and blisters from the evening and walk past where that weirdo with the knife was on the street today, remembering clearly that young woman's face, and final parting glance. This sucks. I need to buy weed and smoke a big fat bone. And I know just where to go. I need to get a bag, get stoned, hit a bar, play some tunes, and forget today. The East Side shops are closed, the traffic's gone and cabs whizz by freely. I slip on my headphones, look to the Walkman in the palm of my hand for an escape. Instead of pushing the play button I scroll the FM radio with my thumb I pass news, sports and weather channels in search for something deeper.

Quinn's place is several blocks down from me on the West Side. I haven't been there in years, but thanks to Teddy, I know he's still dealing there. It's after twelve and the streets are quieter now, car horns are rare, no traffic cops with whistles, only the occasional brother with a boom box passing by. There seems to be more homeless than I've ever seen before on my way over to the West Side. Many bedded down near vents, in church doorways. The sidewalks thin out this time of day, the streets change. It's the people you can't see that are the concern at this time.

A petite blonde woman on the sidewalk up ahead gently kicks the steel cellar door of a small apartment building. As I approach to pass her by, I see she's about five foot four, cute as hell. She kneels down, and speaks to the cellar door in a soft sweet tone.

"C'mon Baby open up, please. I love you baby... can I have some more?"

She looks up at me as I pass; her mascara runs down her cheeks with tears, she's beautiful in a sad way. She's braless in a black leather skirt and a loose red top. Her costume jewelry and high heels confirm she must be coming or going to a club. I keep walking; it's none of my business.

When I step into the doorway of Quinn's five-story walk up, the strong smell of urine almost makes me choke. I'm startled by a man who's sitting against the brick wall in the entry right outside the door. The hair suddenly bristles on my arms and neck. A hypodermic needle sits between his lips, like a bone in his mouth. Tin foil, a spoon, and lighter sit on the ground next to his knee. A scene,

I've never seen. He's sitting among the debris in the doorway with a strip of ragged cloth tied around his arm. Frightened, he nervously stops and gathers his items quickly. I'm cautious of his reaction to my disruption. I gently nudge him with my foot.

"Hey guy, take that crap somewhere else; get lost, man."

His new sneakers, clean jeans, and shirt make me question why he is sitting in this smelly doorway. He doesn't seem homeless or anything like the junkies I've imagined. Without looking up, he quickly gathers his stuff and splits, not a word. I'm sure it wouldn't have been long before someone else would have pissed in here; these doorways are the westside's urinals at night.

I stare for a moment at Quinn's name and apartment number on his mailbox. I'm gonna give it a shot, get a small bag of weed and go to a bar on Ninth Avenue. I buzz his intercom. In a few seconds a static voice comes through the speaker that has a wad of blue gum stuck into it.

"Yeah, who's there?" I think it's him.

"Hey Quinn...It's me Nick." I slip my hand in my front pocket and feel my cash.

"Nick. Nick who?"

My eyes scan the vestibule and address; the attendant booth at the parking lot across the street assures me I'm in the right place. I'm still not sure if it's Quinn though.

"Nick, Patsy's friend from school."

A buzzer sounds, the door unlocks with a loud click, and I walk in. I see the dirty stairs, chipped paint, solid steel spindles, and wooden rail bannister that spiral up five flights I remember well. It's not much different from the building I'm in now. Just he's on the third floor and I'm on the fifth. I tap on his door and I'm let right in. He gives me a solid handshake and a hit on my shoulder. I smell dirt weed and cigarettes.

I'm surprised to see Pauly, Frankie, and Marcos sitting around a coffee table filled with booze and drugs. So much for escaping people I know and the drug scene; Tequila, beer bottles, pot, pipes, pills, magazines, and cocaine create a buffet on the coffee table. I want to turn right around and split before they see me. But part of me is thrilled to see them; it's been so long, and I could use a good laugh. I'm assuming Quinn's special place to cop weed and party back in high school has now become a regular place to party for the boys. Nothing seems to have changed with them, except some of the party material. I see a bag of some pill I don't recognize, and a pile of cocaine on the table.

I'll skip the bar and visit for a while. It looks like everyone's quite comfortable here, like close friends even, not kids from high school anymore. Adult partiers. I'm sure they all, even Frankie, are getting laid by now. *Dream On* by Aerosmith comes on the stereo; it's one I always play on the jukeboxes.

They don't see me as I watch them from across the room. Pauly lowers his head with a straw and inhales a large line of coke off a mirror. I smile inside, this is gonna be a party. I'm glad I don't have to work until three o'clock tomorrow. Pauly leans back and drops the straw; he's pinching his nose in pain. "Yeaahhh, man, owwow!"

He suddenly holds his chest and moves his hand rhythmically like his heart is pumping hard. He takes a big breath and looks up. "Okay, who wants a line?"

"Damn Pauly, those lines are getting bigger and bigger, you're like a vacuum man. I'm gonna call you "Hoover" from now on. They're like twenty-dollar lines man." I hear Frankie say.

"No way dude, a gram is like sixty bucks now. Right Quinn… who wants one?"

"I'll take one, Pauly," Marcos and Pauly look up, surprised as hell. I feel a rush of joy, seeing their happy faces.

Frankie jumps right up slapping me an enthusiastic high five.

"Whoahh…hey Dude. Where you been?" He heads to the fridge and grabs a couple of beers and tosses me one."

"No shit… Nick!" Pauly says, standing up, looking stockier, his hair a bit wilder.

The bottle of Bud is frigid, perfect.

"Hey, Pauly, Marcos… what's up dudes? Cheers!" I crack the beer and raise it up to them.

"Cheers Frank, thanks! I'll take a shot too." Eyeing the Cuervo Gold on the table. "…friggin crazy people on the street today. Must be a full moon or something." I pour some tequila into a plastic cup.

"How come you never friggin call?" Pauly's happy to see me, I feel the same. "You back in New York for a while?" he asks.

"Yeah. Yeah, I am. Took a job in a nice hotel on the East Side." I point to a bag of about ten pills on the coffee table. "What's up with that, what are those things?"

"Ecstasy." Pauly says. "You never saw Ex, dude?" A big smile crosses his face, intriguing me. Marcos's face is not as glad. He points his finger at me and shakes it.

"I heard of it out west. Never saw it."

"Stay clear, Nick, screws with your brain. Pauly ended up making out with a cross-dresser one night." Marcos says.

"Shut up, Marcos. I was so wasted man." Pauly smiles at me. "Nick, it's like tripping but better. You got to try it. All the college chicks are into it."

"Tripping! Pauly? C'mon., not into tripping, dude, but thanks." Pauly's not talking me into this one.

"It's not acid man. It's legal!" he says.

"Totally legal. Five bucks a pill, you want?" Quinn cuts in.

"It's legal…seriously?" I'm curious.

"Don't listen Nick. It's a psychedelic, they're looking to outlaw it." Marcos says. I went to *The Limelight*, one night with him. The place used to be an Episcopal Church; it's just wrong, bro. I felt bad vibes. Some crazy shit, nice girls getting down with total strangers."

I guess the nuns really got to Marcos, he still has his religion. But sex with strangers, I say rock on.

My throat burns, my face distorts, as I swallow the warm tequila. I prefer it chilled. Pauly hands me the straw.

"Help yourself bro." My eyes turn to the lines on the mirror as Marcos exhales a bong hit into the air.

"Damn... Man, it's been so long dude. How's the cooking going? Whatever happened with that place you used to talk about with Gina. What was it a retreat, 'spa', or something right? You doing it?"

"Oh, ehh uh…yeah, oh yeah. I'm working on it still…I'm on it." I'm lying.

As I lower my head to the coke, I realize I haven't done a damn thing towards that plan for many months. I'm not even sure where my notes are.

"Got a little sidetracked with work in LA, but I'm gonna do it… for Gina," I say before I snort.

As the coke lines my nose, my reflection fills its place on the mirror space. I don't like what I see. Steve Tyler is clear as day on the stereo and I pause to catch the lyrics to the song. I've been interested again in lyrics lately. Years ago, Gina and I would listen to songs over and over again to try to learn the words. Unless they were on the album jacket, we wouldn't know them for sure.

I look over to Quinn who's weighing pot in plastic sandwich bags on a small white postage scale in the kitchen. He rolls each up with two hands then licks the very top of the plastic bag, sealing it before he places them neatly into a brown lunch bag.

"Hey, Quinn, I'll take one of those," I say.

He tosses me a bag.

"Twenty-five bucks, that's a half ounce of Jamaican. Cash."

It's okay, smells a bit moldy like dirt weed. I got spoiled in L.A..

Quinn tosses over another bag, it's lighter.

"That's a quarter ounce of Acapulco Gold. Thirty bucks and you got a 'pocket full of gold.' Cash only."

A Mexican dude in Los Angeles told me about the "Acapulco Gold" that's coming out of there now. It's not the same Acapulco Gold that Chaz used to bring us. It's not Acapulco Gold at all. It's regular Mexican weed that turns that color because of *Paraquat*, some chemical the government's spraying on to kill it. They harvest and sell it anyway. The bright golden hue can easily fool you and has, since the late 70's.

"I'll take the Jamaican." I toss the 'Gold' back to Quinn. I don't have the heart to tell him it's toxic and not authentic.

"Here, roll a bone bro." I hand the Jamaican to Marcos. Pauly smacks me on the shoulder.

"Remember that day we were going fishing and stumbled onto the drive-in theater. There wasn't a soul in sight and we broke into the concession stand?"

"*You* broke into the concession stand. It was your idea." I remind him. I have a good buzz kicking in.

"Yeah, but you didn't hesitate grabbing candy and cigarettes." Pauly says.

"You dropped everything when that stray dog chased your ass across the railroad tracks," Marcos reminds me. That frigging dog scared the hell out of me.

"Crazy day, right?" Pauly says.

"Yeah, crazy because you broke into that place to begin with. I'll never forget it, I lost the fishing pole my Dad gave me that day." He died the year before.

"Oh yeah. You lost your pole in the woods somewhere." Pauly says.

"Here, bro," Marcos throws me the joint he rolled.

"What's this? A toothpick?" I forgot how thin we rolled joints in New York. I hold it up to Pauly.

"Come on, dude. What's with the pin joint?" He says to Marcos. "There's plenty of pot."

"That's a nice bone, dude. What are you talking about? It's gonna burn good, even."

Pauly's going full swing with the coke. He hands me the straw, again, I don't hesitate to suck it up. It's a little after 1 AM, and I'm here for the duration.

I won't be sleeping anytime soon, so, might as well go with the flow.

"So, Pauly's making out with transvestites now, huh?" I ask Marcos.

Marcos shakes his head. "We pulled him off. I'm still not sure he wanted us to. That pill can lead to strange things."

"So, 'Romeo', that ecstasy sounds like a walk on the wild side. Not interested."

But count me in on the next gram of blow.

Chapter Fourteen

Fooling Yourself

"How can you be such an angry young man,
when your future looks quite bright to me"

~ Styx

IT'S 4:30 AM AND THE high-pitched synthesizers in the STYX song on Quinn's stereo start to grate on me like they have never done before. Maybe it's because I'm at the stage of my high where I'm not liking it, I'm wired. This chair is getting uncomfortable. I look to put my feet up, but first I reach for the tequila and pour a shot hoping to bring me down. I wolf it down and plop my feet up on the coffee table. Within minutes they're back on the floor, as I lean forward into the chaos on the coffee table to inhale another line.

My eyes strain to stay focused as I lift my head from the table. There's just booze, ashtrays, pills, pot, and bongs as far as my eyes can see. I feel convicted…guilty. Screwed up again. I'm heading for a sleepless night before work. It's been a while and it's not good. I debate taking coke to work to get through the shift. I don't want to take the risk, but I may have to.

Pauly, is so high. Like I've never seen him before. He's slid into the armchair, like he's melded to it. His hands and elbows lay immobile above him on the armrests. His hair is disheveled, eyes leering suspiciously, and there's a white crust of coke around his nostrils.

I laugh, to myself. The irony, he's thinking the same thing, I bet. I check my nose for crusted coke with my pinky finger. He's never seen me this high either. Weed was our drug of choice when I left for the west coast.

Our first buzz was in junior high, I remember. We snuck beers from Pauly's house into the woods after school. I didn't even like the taste, I wanted to spit it out, but we made sure we all drank it. I'd spill some when no one was watching so they'd think I liked it.

Then came the buzz, the giddiness; the laughter.

So, the next time my taste buds said spit it out— I forced it down instead, looking for that laughter. Just a quart between two of us used to be enough. Then it was a quart each. Then an eight pack each and a joint by the time we were in ninth grade. The brandy and schnapps came out each winter. The booze burning down my throat was tolerated, expecting a payoff.

Now after several shots of warm Cuervo even that tastes sweet. I pour another.

"Hey, Nick what's up with Chaz? Haven't heard anything from that dude either," asks Marcos, as he peels cards from a deck, lining them up for another round of solitaire.

'He's gay.' Would be the easy answer, but I hold back. Doesn't matter, he was straight with me. "Honestly, dude…I don't know. He was doing well in school. But I moved out, closer to my job after Gina passed. We haven't kept in touch much."

My eyes turn to Pauly again and my father comes to mind. He didn't like me hanging with him. Or Phil and some of the guys as we got older, he heard about them getting into trouble. But I'd known them since grade school and they weren't bad then.

Now, seeing the guys a bit stupefied, zombielike, staring at a toxic table, grazing it, when their appetite acts up is a bit bothersome. The music plays, I quit thinking so much, and try to catch the lyrics to the Styx song. I give up within a minute as the synthesizers start to annoy me again.

Quinn holds up the bottle of tequila and a shot glass, offering it to anyone who'll take it.

"One day I'm going to make the deal to end all deals," he says. "I'm telling you, no more of this nickel and dime crap. One big mother boatload, the grand transfer —then I'll sit back and have a crew of dudes selling this stuff for me." Pauly arises.

"I'll buy that boatload dude, when I hit the lottery. I've been doing the math, gonna have the numbers figured out. Right now, the ponies at OTB are being good to me. I study the odds, know how to pick 'em." Pauly's speech is starting to slur.

"Get a job, Pauly, betting on horses "Off Track" is no career dude." Marcos says.

"I got a job," he mumbles back.

Now Marcos, my dad always liked, since we were little. He was always polite, respectful. We'd sometimes see him in mass, on his own, and my dad would always invite him over for Sunday dinner. It looks like he's still not into pills, coke, or anything. He just really likes his weed. Good for him.

"Being a 'bookie' is NOT a job dude," Frankie cuts in as he reaches for the bong.

"It sure as hell is! Ya know how much I made with football sheets last year, bro?" he says.

"Seriously, Pauly. Get a real job, like me." Marcos proudly states.

He slips on dark sunglasses, his smile's wide and white.

"My future's so bright at UPS, bro... I bought these shades for that sunny day when I get out of the warehouse and have my own truck route." He really looks sharp with them on — you no longer see he's cockeyed.

Pauly starts leering around again. He quickly places his finger over his lips. "Sssshhh...shhhuush! You hear that?" He turns towards the wall and whispers. "Voices next door."

"I don't hear anything," Frankie says.

Pauly sniffs loudly, inhaling the coke in his nostrils. Forgetting his own warning, to be silent. "Seriously...shh, snff." He looks through the window. "Shut the shades, bro. They're watching us."

Nobody moves, and we just look at each other and smile. Pauly jumps up, pulls the shade down, and goes to the door to make sure it's locked. Again, he turns to us with his finger on his lips. "Ssshhh."

He walks over to the wall and puts his ear up against it. We all just look at him and then at each other and start cracking up.

"Pauly… you are buggin' bro," Quinn says.

"Yeah you think so? Maybe, but I swear…"

Frankie offers me the bong and I pass.

Pauly becomes awfully quiet. His shifty eyes look around madly. Then he drops his head into another line and quickly slugs his beer.

"H-h-hey Quinn, you sure your phone ain't bugged? I swear I-I heard a cli-clicking noise the other day." His slur begins to stammer.

"Dude, you're 'bugged' man, relax. Wanna Quaalude?" Quinn says.

Marcos takes his afro pick out and starts teasing his fro– his attention turns from Pauly to me. His hair looks like an impressive beach ball of fine steel wool, light and airy. Like a young Michael Jackson, before all the weird stuff.

"So what's the latest with that biz plan you were working on anyway, some resort place, I remember, right? What's up with that?" he asks. I'm caught off guard, tongue tied.

"Yeah, yeah man sure… I'm uh, uhm, I'm telling you, this place I've been planning it'll cost people like three bills a night, yeah, like three hundred. It'll have an in-house movie theatre, gourmet kitchen, masseuse, sauna and stuff, all included.

And every night there'll be a cocktail party with passed hors d'oeuvres and live music before dinner." I begin recollecting the concept.

"A movie theater in the place. Cool, very cool. How many seats?" Quinn asks and I don't know.

"Uhm..like a hundred…yeah. I catered in a lot of homes in LA that have movie theaters right in their house, bro. Screening rooms, so cool. I'm gonna do that but bigger."

I start winging it; my mind is on overdrive.

"And we'll show great movies like *Debbie Does Dallas* and *Deep Throat*. And after the movie, we'll do bongs and blow, eat hash brownies, and hit the sauna, steam room, and Jacuzzi. There'll be babes everywhere... I'll show Hugh Heffner how to party," I say, rolling right out of my mouth, like it was on the tip of my tongue.

"Whoa, dude, where'd that come from?" Marcos asks, as I think the same thing.

"Sounds cool. I'm in. But *Debbie does Dallas?* C'mon you gotta screen the latest porn flicks. I can get them, I know a guy." Quinn says.

Pauly perks up at the sound of porn. "Re-Remember in eighth grade, dude? ...when Ph-Philly was looking for his dad's stash of speed and h-he found his guns and porn instead? He had those videotapes, they were awesome bro!"

Frankie's looking right at me, I bet he still gets proofed. His baby face is semi-encircled by the raised collar on his alligator shirt. He looks surprised at me, shaking his head, with a look like he wants to say something.

"You got something to say, Frank?" I beat him to the punch.

He sits straight up and looks right at me. His preppy gaze seems to intimidate, backed by his college attendance, and professional law ambitions. I take him more seriously.

"Yeah, I do...what the hell, Nick? I'm not so sure that was in Gina's plan. And I don't think her dad would be psyched her dream turned into a porn place." He's not holding back.

"That sounds more like swapping at Plato's Retreat or in the Poconos now," he says.

Her dad? Man...why did he have to go and bring up her dad?

"Why don't you open a peep show too? What the hell." Marcos adds sarcastically.

"I'll have you a job in Times Square in no time bro. You learn the ropes first by mopping up the booths." Quinn says with a chuckle. "But there's no doubt big money in that biz and it's only growing."

Pauly laughs out loud with Quinn, then catches himself, and quickly shuts up. His eyes begin leering, over his shoulder.

"What the hell happened to you, dude?" Frankie says with a scowl.

"Hey, what the…what do you mean by that?" I'm starting to sweat this.

"Forget about it." Frankie looks away.

Pauly cuts in, his speech robbed by the blow. His jaw now rotating from the effect of the coke as he attempts words, "Re-re-remember, Nick? Damn m-m-man that's some g-g-good stuff. I-I always wanted to partner y' know…Re-remember, bro? "I'll run the slots, roulette and p-p-poker tables too," he says.

He hesitates, his jaw now grinding like a llama; he looks at the door suspiciously. "Hey is..is th..that locked?"

"Geez Pauly. Lay off the lines man. You're paranoid," Marcos says.

"Hey Pauly, just because you're paranoid, doesn't mean they're not out to get you! Y'know." Quinn says.

Marcos laughs with Quinn. But I'm not laughing. And neither is Frank. I want to know what's up with him, what's his gripe. I'm not ready to 'forget about it'.

"No, really, what do you mean by that Frankie…what are you saying?"

Frankie looks to the floor. "Nothing, forget about it, I said."

"No, I won't forget about it. C'mon, you got a problem with me?"

"Let it go, Nick. Just drop it," Marcos says.

"No, no I won't let it go," My nerves are up, never had a problem with Frankie. "What's your problem, Frank? You don't like girls, skin flicks?"

He looks me square in the eye. Far from the shy kid I remember growing up with.

"Okay...okay, you wanna know my problem?" His finger pointing right at me, "You. You are a problem." He sits up in his chair. "Don't come off like you're gonna do this for Gina. That's a bunch of crap. You haven't done a thing for Gina." Marcos sits up.

"Lay off Frankie... keep cool bro. Let it go," Marcos says.

"No. No, screw that Marcos. She was the kindest girl in school; the coolest and first class. We all knew her as a close friend from way back, ya know."

My blood heats up, as I wonder what he's getting to, unsure how to respond. The pressure moves to my head, which now aches, as he lays into me.

"What? I haven't done crap for her? She broke up with me man. She started dating friggin' Patsy."

"That's bull Nick. You know it. You suck. That 'spa' plan was her dream too. She was so excited about it, about the future, about life. She told me all about it man. We talked a lot, and that idea was cool, it was all good. But you changed, bro. Over time you soured. And then what did you do? Knock her up, run away, and forget about her. And now that dream turns into a porn show? What's up with that?"

My head wants to explode, but I take the hits. They cut bad, really bad, coming from him. And he's right. As if crashing from the coke this time in the morning isn't bad enough.

"C'mon Frankie. She broke up with me."

"Yeah right. You changed over the year's bro, and not for the better. You were the coolest couple, since I can remember. I envied you. Not now, no way. I never saw her so bummed out."

"She was pissed at me, dude. I tried calling; she never called back. And she never said she was pregnant."

"She didn't? That's not what I heard." Frankie says. "You didn't even go to her funeral, man. That was wrong, so, wrong, in so many ways. It's been all about you for years."

"He's right, Nick. I heard you took off on her and Patsy told me you never went to her funeral, man," Quinn says.

"Shut the hell up! Screw you, Quinn. I had to work a real job. You and your damn brother can go to hell." A serious rage builds in me and I feel I may snap and want to kill someone. "Screw you all. I'm outta here. My day was bad enough. Where is Patsy anyway? I wanna kick his ass."

"He stopped by for weed right before you came. Right, Quinn?" Marcos says.

"Yeah, yeah, weed. That's right," says Quinn.

"He just got released from prison a couple of months ago. He hasn't gotten over the accident. Doing some hard drugs, I hear." Marcos says.

I can't wait to get out the door. Marcos pops up from his chair.

"Hey, don't lose your cool, brother. Come together, keep the peace," Marcos says.

Frankie's not finished and a bit calmer. "You know Nick, I wish I said something. You know, spoke up, and maybe asked her out. I wanted to, so bad. I hated seeing her with Patsy. I stood back when I should have stood up. But I sure didn't want to see her with you again either, after the way you split. She deserved better. The world was better with her here; it's not the same. I miss her." I didn't know he thought like this, but I do know how he feels now that she's gone.

Pauly's leaning down into another monster-size line of coke.

Marcos' eyes bulge. "Cool it, Pauly. Lay off that crap. I'm serious"

"N-n-no worries, br-br-bro, I got this for free."

"Just because it's free doesn't mean it can't kill you, dude." Marcos says.

I look at them all and feel disgusted, with myself, my life. I wish I was dead, not her.

I really wish Frankie had the balls to ask her out when he thought of it. He's a good guy, gonna be a lawyer. And he's right; she deserved better. I head for the door and Quinn stops me.

"You owe me twenty-five bucks, bro," he says.

As I hand him his money, he shoves a bag in my hand.

"Here's several Quaaludes, on me. It'll help you sleep."

I push them into my pocket and take a look around his place. If I just went to Columbus Circle and bought weed, this never would have happened. I'm shaky. I wanna do another shot. But I want out of here more. I need to get far from this place.

Marcos's eyes meet mine. "Peace." I nod. "Don't let me down." He says sincerely.

Thoughts of Gina have my mind all twisted. Nobody's ever loved me like she did.

I shut the door hard behind me and head down the steps onto the street— into the darkest depths of morning, that time when I dread the dawn's light.

I don't remember how I got from the door of Quinn's building to the entrance of an alley but that's what I'm looking into. The area is dark and vile. Trash is piled high and dumpsters are overflowing. Water drips from a broken drainpipe smacking the black plastic garbage bags and runs down the alley. There are no streetlights on the other side. As my eyes adjust I look further into the alley. I feel I'm not alone…and I'm right.

"Looks like you had a rough night, son," I hear someone say behind me.

Startled, I turn and see under the glimmer of a distant streetlight, a burly man in jeans and a leather vest with sky blue eyes. His skullcap, vest, silver-grey ponytail, and bushy white goatee say, sturdy old biker. *What the hell does he want?*

"No, no I'm cool, just hanging out, heading home." His wide shoulders and strong arms hold a heavy steel chain in hand.

233

"You looking to take a shortcut home?" the guy says to me. "cos that isn't the best one. And if you choose that path, it's the long way home and you're gonna have to take what comes with it."

"What are you talking about, man?" I look back at the guy.

I hear snarling and a low growl. Suddenly that damn dog that's been hounding me comes around from behind him. It sits eagerly next to him, staring at me with lit, fiery eyes.

"Hey...hey, what's up with your dog, man?"

"Not mine. He's yours, you just keep feeding him like you have been and there's no stopping him."

"He's not my dog, man." I insist.

"He sure is. He was the runt, didn't have a chance years ago, but you fed him well. Now that's all he wants, more and more. He's insatiable."

The dog's eyes are focused, frightening, and watching my every move. It snarls, baring its teeth as it steps toward me, still restrained by the guy holding it back with the chain leash.

"He's not mine, I don't want him. You keep that thing away from me," I say, stepping away, deeper into the darkness of the alley.

"Sorry, no can do. He's all yours now." The dog lunges pulling the thick chain taught with teeth bared. The silver haired man pulls the animal back to heel with both arms. He slowly bends over and reluctantly, releases the animal's thick steel collar from the leash.

I turn and run further into the darkness, and within several steps, I trip over somebody's legs in blue jeans and sneakers and stumble to the ground. They're passed out, face down in a garbage bag. The dog's eyes are fixed on me, as it slowly approaches, unleashed, and baring its teeth.

I think it's the junkie I kicked out from Quinn's doorway. I got to bolt, get away, but I can't leave this guy here, face down in a plastic bag.

I nudge him with my foot. "Get up man…get up! We got to get out of here." A strong urine smell hits my noise stronger than the stench in the alley. His stud earring is a diamond, like mine. He just lies limp, motionless and I hope he's breathing. I roll him over. Foams frothing from the side of his open mouth, and then dead man's eyes meet mine. They're rolled so far back I only see whites. *Damn man.* My mind races as I'm alarmed by the hound's snarling approach. My heart pounds in my chest as I become terrified. I jolt up and run to the darkness for comfort, for somewhere to hide, anywhere to escape this mad dog. I run, every pore sweating profusely as I look and see it lunge over the dead man in pursuit of me. Fear consumes me and I succumb, into a dark oblivion.

Beeeep…beeeeep…beeeeep…beeep…beep. My breath is shallow and labored; the whole left side of my body is numb, motionless. I lift my working fingers to my throbbing forehead and smooth them through my hair. I'm wet with sweat. *What's beeping?*

My skin feels cold, clammy, and I can't seem to stop my eyes from tearing, blurring my vision. I roll over and can faintly see wavy lines on a monitor screen. I squint at the light breaking into the room through the blinds of a window. Painfully I try to move closer but my whole side is immobile and my muscles ache. I scrape my parched tongue between cracked, dry lips. I'm extremely thirsty.

Beeeep…beeeeep…beep… The beeping noise is getting louder. *Where am I?* I stretch toward the blind and push it aside. Through foggy eyes I see a *U-Haul* truck in reverse on the street below, the beeping, it's warning signal.

I roll back over as a prickling sensation travels up my left side, and the numbness fades. I stare at my ceiling. My thoughts spin me back to last night, Quinn's place, and the dream I just woke from, sticks in my mind, as clear as day.

I'm pretty sure Quinn's Quaaludes had something to do with it. I

235

took two. I did get some sleep, I guess. My alarm clock reads two in the afternoon— I have an hour before work. My mind is hazy, my nerves shaking. *Why do I do what I don't want to do?*

I climb down from the loft and guzzle the half empty glass of warm water sitting on an end table. I pick up the phone next to it and dial, as I stare into the wavy lines on the TV screen. The phone rings on the other end.

"Hello…" her voice calms my nerves.

"Hi Ma. Hey, yeah uhmm, I was just thinking …ehem, how's dinner with the family at the Hawaiian Luau place sound to you, it's been a long time. Maybe early next week?" I'm, trying hard to keep a strong, clear voice. "We could, um.. catch up on things." Seconds of dead silence are broken by her tearful sniffle and sigh.

"Yes. Yes, certainly. That sounds just wonderful honey. And yes, it has been a long time."

Author's Note

Life is not easy. It's not meant to be. It's not always fair.
But we were built to persevere, to overcome, and to thrive,
to live on.
We all have our own story and are in various chapters of life.
What chapter is Hounding you? What demons are you
dealing with?
Depression? Alcohol? Opiods? Pornography? Suicide? AIDS?
Pregnancy?
Homelessness? Domestic abuse? Sex trafficking? LGBT con-
cerns/support?

Nothing and no one can possess your will, your spirit. Its power is
beyond measure.
You are the author of the book of your life. Circumstances are
temporary.
You have the power to write your next chapter. Dare to dream big,
to make a difference.
Or… leave it incomplete.
It may end up a sad, short story. But I assure you there is someone
in hard times that needs to hear your whole story.
So, make it good, your Co-Author is within you, waiting.
Tap into that Love, Wisdom, receive the Grace and fear not.
Then watch the miracle of a wonderful life unfold.
Yours!

*There's a spotlight waiting, No matter who you are, 'Cause every-
body's got a song to sing... ...everyone's a star.*

~ The Righteous Brothers

The Hound of Heaven
Into the Pit

The coming chapters in Book Two

If you are in a crisis, please…

…look over the following pages. Make a call or go online and be encouraged by compassionate, supportive people who understand. They are waiting to help you begin another chapter, your success story. Your story will then be someone's hope, a story of triumph, reuniting families and friends. Do it to heal yourself, and others. And you'll live forever gratefully in their hearts

What If I Am Afraid to Call?

Making the call to a drug abuse hotline can seem overwhelming. Picking up the phone takes courage, and it is the first step towards healing.

The hotline is staffed by specialists who want to help. They are dedicated to providing helpful information, treatment options, and answers.

You will not be judged. Addiction is a disorder that can be overcome, and you can call as many times as you need. Supportive individuals are standing by right now to assist you. It can be difficult to make the telephone call, but you can do it. There are no risks or obligations.

About the DrugAbuse.com— Each year, the DrugAbuse.com hotline connects thousands of people with substance abuse treatment programs throughout the U.S. toll-free. Calls are answered by American Addiction Centers (AAC) who have treatment support specialists available 24/7, 365 days a year.

Both our treatment directory and our hotline are offered at no cost to you.

Where Else Can I Find Help?

National Hotlines:

SAMHSA Facility Locator - http://findtreatment.samhsa.gov/index. html 1-800-662-HELP (4357) Free and confidential information in English and Spanish for individuals and family members facing substance abuse and mental health issues. 24 hours a day, 7 days a week.

Suicide Prevention Lifeline - http://www.suicidepreventionlifeline. org/ 1-800-273-TALK (8255) 24-hour, toll-free, confidential suicide prevention hotline available to anyone in suicidal crisis or emotional distress. Your call is routed to the nearest crisis center in the national network of more than 150 crisis centers.

American Association of Poison Control Centers - http://www.aap-cc.org/ For a poisoning emergency in the U.S. call 1-800-222-1222 The American Association of Poison Control Centers supports the nation's 55 poison centers in their efforts to prevent and treat poison exposures. Poison centers offer free, confidential medical advice 24 hours a day, seven days a week

Nonprofit Treatment Centers:

Betty Ford Center - http://www.bettyfordcenter.org/index.php

Phoenix House - http://www.phoenixhouse.org/

Caron - http://www.caron.org/

Odyssey House - http://www.odysseyhouse.org/

Recovery Gateway - http://recovergateway.org/

Dawn Farm - http://dawnfarm.org/

Austin Recovery - http://www.austinrecovery.org/

Recovery Programs:

Alcoholics Anonymous - http://www.aa.org/

Narcotics Anonymous - http://www.na.org/

Smart Recovery - http://www.smartrecovery.org/

Additional Drug Abuse Hotline Resources

The following hotline numbers are presented here as additional resources. If you are facing an immediate crisis, please call emergency services at 911.

- **Boys Town National Hotline**
- 1 (800) 448-3000
- Crisis and resource line staffed by counselors to provide information about a variety of issues, including chemical dependency.

- **Covenant House Teen Hotline (NineLine)**
- 1 (800) 999-9999
- General hotline for adolescents, teens and their families. Assistance with any kind of problem – including alcohol and drug abuse. Covenant House specializes in homeless and runaway youth.

- **National Council on Alcoholism and Drug Dependence, Inc. (NCADD)**
- 1 (800) NCA-CALL (622-2255)
- NCADD's HOPE LINE directs callers to numerous affiliate programs around the country to assist, at a local level, with substance abuse issues.

- **National Institute on Drug Abuse (NIDA)**
- 1 (800) 662-HELP (4357)
- National agency dedicated to prevention of drug abuse, and treatment of existing drug problems. Round the clock help in finding local drug treatment centers.

- **Substance Abuse and Mental Health Services Administration (SAMHSA) National Helpline**
- 1 (800) 662-HELP (4357)
- 1 (800) 487-4889 (TDD) for hearing impaired
- Confidential information service for individuals and family members faced with substance abuse disorders and/or mental health issues. Information available in English and Spanish.
- **National Suicide Prevention Lifeline**
- 1 (800) 273-TALK (8255)
- Not just a suicide hotline. Offers help with issues of drug and alcohol abuse
- **The Partnership at Drugfree.org**
- 1 (855) DRUG-FREE (378-4373)

Not a crisis line, but provides information to parents about adolescent and teen drug abuse, prevention and treatment.

Many state government websites will also provide local drug and alcohol resources to those in need. To find your state government's website, do a web search for your state name and '.gov'. Once your state website is located, substance abuse resources shouldn't be hard to find and should provide further phone contacts for assistance.

You will not be judged. Addiction is a disorder that can be overcome, and you can call as many times as you need. Supportive individuals are standing by right now to assist you. It can be difficult to make the telephone call, but you can do it. There are no risks or obligations.

Want to listen to "Nicks Mix" from *The Hound of Heaven - Book One* and follow the music in his journey to *L.A. and back*, the songs he tuned into along the way.

 Hound of Heaven Book 1 "Nicks Mix"
14 songs, 59.7 minutes, 57.5 MB

Name	Time	Album	Artist
1 Knockin' On Heaven's Door	2:30	The Essential Bob Dylan	Bob Dylan
2 Eighteen	3:02		Alice Cooper
3 Baba O'Riley	5:13		The Who
4 No Time	3:44		The Guess Who
5 Goin To California	3:36		Led Zepplin
6 Long Time	7:52		Boston
7 God Only Knows	2:59		Brian Wilson
8 Highway To Hell	3:32		AC/DC
9 Runnin With The Devil	3:41		Van Halen
10 Lola	4:52		Kinks
11 Fire and Rain	3:30		James Taylor
12 Living Years	5:38		Mike and the Mechanics
13 Dream On	4:30		Aerosmith
14 Foolin yourself	5:14		Styx

To go even deeper, read the song lyrics in "Nick's Mix."

"Then you listen to the music and you like to sing along,
You want to get the meaning out of each and every song,
Then you find yourself a message and some words to call your own
and take 'em home."

~Bread

Lyric websites:

www.azlyrics.com

www.genius.com

www.lyrics.com

www.metrolyrics.com

The Hound of Heaven is a novel that pays homage to the musicians that Nick journeys with through his story. It is with respect and gratitude we honor and share their website links with you.

www.bobdylan.com

www.alicecooper.com

www.thewho.com

www.theguesswho.com

www.ledzeppelin.com

www.bandboston.com

www.thebeachboys.com

www.acdc.com

www.van-halen.com

www.thekinks.info

www.jamestaylor.com

mikeandthemechanics.com

www.aerosmith.com

styxworld.com/

A note in honor of the 1880's opioid addicted poet who penned the title.

With gratitude and credit to author Pat McNamara-

Francis Thompson and the "Hound of Heaven"

By Pat McNamara
It's a poem that every Catholic schoolchild knew once upon a time. Eugene O'Neill could recite Francis Thompson's "Hound of Heaven" from memory, and J.R.R. Tolkien was an admirer of it. G.K. Chesterton considered Thompson one of the great English poets, a "shy volcano." Although Victorian poetry may be out of fashion today, many still find comfort in Thompson's image of a loving God relentlessly pursuing the wayward soul:

> *I fled Him, down the nights and down the days;*
> *I fled Him, down the arches of the years;*
> *I fled Him, down the labyrinthine ways*
> *Of my own mind; and in the mist of tears*
> *I hid from Him, and under running laughter.*
> *Up vistaed hopes I sped;*
> *And shot, precipitated,*
> *Adown Titanic glooms of chasmèd fears,*
> *From those strong Feet that followed, followed after.*
> *But with unhurrying chase,*
> *And unperturbèd pace,*
> *Deliberate speed, majestic instancy,*
> *They beat-and a Voice beat*
> *More instant than the Feet-*
> *"All things betray thee, who betrayest Me."*

What many didn't know was that this poem, hailed as one of the great Catholic poems, was the product of a deeply troubled soul, a man who battled addiction, poverty and depression throughout his adult life.

He started off in life rather comfortably, a doctor's son in northern England. The oldest of three, he grew up a shy introverted child with a strong love for the classics, especially Shakespeare. Some biographers have suggested there was something about young Thompson that made it doubtful whether he would ever "make it" in the "real world."

As a young boy, he attended Ushaw College, a recently founded Catholic school in northern England. It was thought that he might pursue the priesthood, but his frail health precluded it. His father wanted him to enter medical school, which he did. But deep in his heart, Francis knew that this wasn't his calling either. As an early biographer writes, he "made a pretense of study" for six years. However, he never practiced medicine.

Instead, an inner voice was drawing him toward a literary life, and to London. He started off as a bookseller, at which he was less than successful. For a while he worked in a shoemaker's store before he ended up homeless on the streets of London. For three years, he sold matches, called cabs, begged for his subsistence, and fought a growing drug habit. He found some solace in the public libraries, but he was banned for his ragged appearance. A peer wrote:

A stranger figure than Thompson's was not to be seen in London. Gentle in looks, half-wild in externals, his face worn by pain and the fierce reactions of laudanum, his hair and straggling beard neglected, he had yet a distinction and aloofness of bearing that marked him in the crowd; and when he opened his lips he spoke as a gentleman and a scholar. It was impossible and unnecessary to think always of the tragic side of his life.

At one point, he attempted suicide. But a London prostitute took him in, gave him a place to stay, and looked after him for a while. Thompson never revealed her name, but he would later refer to her as his savior.

In 1887, he sent some poems to Wilfrid Meynell, editor of a Catholic literary magazine titled *Merry England*. Thompson apologized "for the soiled state of the manuscript. It is due, not to slovenliness, but to the strange places and circumstances under which it has been written."

Meynell published Thompson's poems. Once he became aware of Thompson's situation, he helped the poet get back on his feet and kick his drug habit. He arranged for Thompson to recuperate at a monastery. Meynell and other friends looked after him for the remaining years of his life. Physically, however, he never quite recovered from life on the street.

During these years he wrote highly regarded poems and essays. He was called "a poet of high thinking, of 'celestial vision,' and of imaginings that found literary images of answering splendour." But all agreed that none surpassed "The Hound of Heaven," which one critic called "one of the great odes of which the English language can boast." The end of the poem describes the wandering soul's final surrender to God's love:

> *Now of that long pursuit,*
> *Comes at hand the bruit;*
> *That Voice is round me like a bursting sea:*
> *"And is thy Earth so marred,*
> *Shattered in shard on shard?*
> *Lo, all things fly thee, for thou fliest Me.*
> *Strange, piteous, futile thing;*
> *Wherefore should any set thee love apart?*

Seeing none but I makes much of naught" (He said),
"And human love needs human meriting;
How hast thou merited –
Of all Man's clotted clay, the dingiest clot?
Alack! Thou knowest not
How little worthy of any love thou art!
Whom wilt thou find to love ignoble thee,
Save Me, save only Me?
All which I took from thee, I did but take,
Not for thy harms,
But just that thou might'st seek it in My arms,
All which thy child's mistake
Fancies as lost, I have stored for thee at home –
Rise, clasp My hand, and come!"
Halts by me that footfall:
Is my gloom, after all,
Shade of His hand, outstretched caressingly?
"Ah, fondest, blindest, weakest,
I am He Whom thou seekest!
Thou dravest love from thee, who dravest Me."

Over time, poor health caught up with Thompson, and on the morning of November 13, 1907, he died of tuberculosis. The restless, gentle soul was finally at peace. Although the story of his addiction was long kept hidden, knowing the full story of Francis Thompson only provides a greater resonance to his work. For ultimately his story is not one of despair but of hope and triumph. Author Michael Daniel notes:

In an age such as ours in which drug addiction and writings emanating from it are symptomatic of nihilism, and ultimately of despair, Thompson's moving poetry, resonating with a Catholic worldview of hope, provides a positive alternative.

Written by Pat McNamara

To hear the infamous haunting poem, "The Hound of Heaven," recited by the late great Richard Burton...

On **Youtube** search for: **Richard Burton The Hound of Heaven.**

Contact or Join us at:

www.facebook.com/PulpoPublishing

www.thehoundofheavennovel.com

pulpopublishing@gmail.com

Empty Pages

~Traffic~

Start Your Life's Next Chapter Here

* * * * *

"For I know the plans I have for you," declares the Lord, "plans to prosper you and not to harm you, plans to give you hope and a future."

~Jeremiah 29:11 (NIV)

About the Author

Joseph A. Rispoli has written extensively for many years; memoirs, journals, screenplays and novels were personal and never open to be published, until now. His debut novel The Hound of Heaven— 'No man can serve two masters' is the first book in a promising series of fiction.

His busy long weeks as a chef in New York City changed when he was personally selected to be a live-in private chef for Brian Wilson of the Beach Boys. It was there, in Malibu, he found time to explore creative writing. Troubled by seeing dependency firsthand, he became determined to reach those who struggle with addictions, and believes the power of music and story can do so.

He's the youngest of eight siblings raised in Rockland County, New York. His love for the culinary arts has opened doors to some of the finest kitchens in NY and LA, and to the addictions that can be acquired in them. He enjoys mentoring upcoming chefs with his culinary insights, positive outlook and personal stories. He encourages them to write their next chapters in life and to make each one better than the last.

He resides in the tristate area of Manhattan with his lovely wife Laurie and enjoys the tempo of the city as well as the still sounds of the country and traveling. He cherishes time with his large extended family and enjoys making memories and meals with them often. Especially around the holidays.

Acknowledgments

I'd be mistaken not to thank all the critics, naysayers and negative voices that doubted me throughout this journey. The loudest one being within my head. Without them, I never would have extended beyond my reach to find the Source of this dream and the strength needed to dissolve the doubt, confirm the vision, and nurture my patience through the long process. Thank you all. The peace of mind you drove me to find is priceless, beyond all understanding. And I thank God for you.

~

That said, I take great pleasure in acknowledging those who I am truly grateful to, who believed and contributed in so many ways to support this vision.

~

For my wonderful wife Laurie, who has been there all the steps of the way. Through my frustrations, rewrites, rejections and uncertainties, her input, love and support throughout this means more than she may ever know.

~

Garrett De Temple a fan of the story from the very first draft. He encouraged me to take different narrative approaches to find the best fit for the story. His professional editing, advice, notes and patience with me, a fledgling author, was certainly appreciated, I consider him a true friend.

~

Author Marianne De Pierres, my Australian friend and houseguest who edited with great efficiency and insight, she shared it needed a few more rounds to improve, encouraging me to carry on when I wanted to give in. She suggested I read more fiction and handed me an American classic my rough work reminded her of *On the Road* by Jack Kerouac.

~

To the friends, family and authors who have read, proofread or shared notes over the course of this adaption from screenplay to novel; Pam McWilliams, Maureen Sherry, Gary Palermo, Marian Armstrong, Chanelle

260

Williams, Mary Buonocore, Father George Torock, Dina Cahill Wolleben Virginia Lago, Mark Van Sise, Msgnr Jim Conlan (deceased), Francis Rispoli, Joe Capone, Sami Assad, Jerald Boak, Nick Vara, Dean Dellolio, Michael Mindes, James Mulligan, Vin Annunziata, Ron Firestone, my whole family and many others who in ways shared input or listened patiently as I bent their ears with songs and story over and over again.

~

A sincere thanks to my brother Michael, a celebrated actor who gifted me early on with input and writing lessons. He encouraged me to learn the craft, do the work needed and to write the story only I can see.

~

Thanks to the talented illustrator James Madsen, who worked so patiently designing the cover, to Betsy Franco Feeney for cover copy placement and logo work, Clark Kenyon for his book formatting and eBook contribution. A big thank you to Al Ryan of Ryan printing Inc., for his support in getting the first copies into my hand through designer Dave Zilkowski who completed the finishing work for the interior and first edition cover.

~

And to the musicians—many songs are in fact stories of trials and triumphs. Through music, hope can appear, inspire, and change lives. Perhaps even save one.

Thank you.